# Choose Courage in Your Relationships:

# Profit From Problems

### by Ruth M. Schimel, Ph.D.

### Career & Life Management Consultant

# DON'T MISS THIS GROUNDBREAKING BOOK THAT PROVIDES THE FOUNDATION FOR THE HANDBOOKS
## *Choose Courage: Step Into the Life You Want*

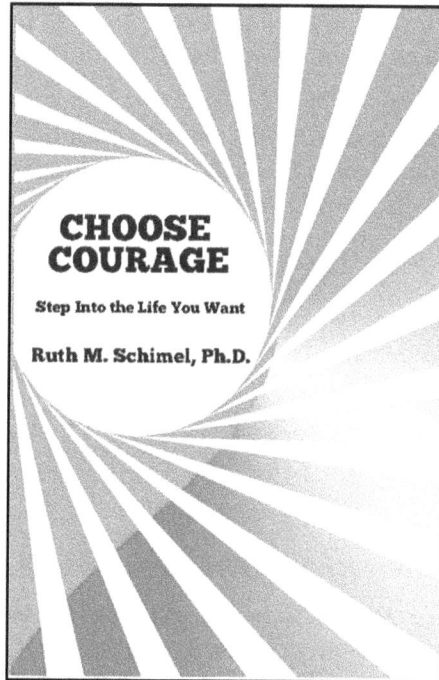

## by Ruth M. Schimel, Ph.D.
## Career & Life Management Consultant

## Available at www.amazon.com or through neighborhood bookstores
### In paperback and Kindle editions

Choose Courage: Step Into the Life You Want

## ACCLAIM FOR CHOOSE COURAGE

*We are in the era as never before where individuals can express who they are, what they believe in, what they seek, and where to move forward across most of the globe.*

*Technology has enabled and empowered the ability to have a platform to express your opinion (from Tweets to blog posts, to other means). Thus the timely publication of the Dr. Ruth Schimel's new book entitled "Choose Courage: Step Into the Life You Want" is ideal to guide individuals to not only pursue their dreams but also to realize them.*

*Choose Courage offers a unique set of guidelines that is sensitive to the individual reader and allows everyone to tailor the recommendations to their own set of circumstances. Most "How-to Books" dictate a lofty set of rules and principles to the reader for the pathway to success. Dr. Schimel offers a positive, manageable, and realistic process.*

*Choose Courage is an outstanding life map that guides a range of individuals from business leaders to elementary teachers to exhibit their courage and to use their respective talents without boundaries, without fear.*

**Dr. Hubert Glover, Drexel University, Author of *Giraffes of Technology: The Making of the 21st Century Leader***

## USE AND BENEFITS OF CHOOSE COURAGE

***Choose Courage: Step Into the Life You Want*** **transforms what could be a heroic cliché into concrete ways you can realize your true capacities. Based on doctoral-level research with everyday people, the book provides a 21st century definition of courage. The array of tools and guidance will help you build on your strengths and skills as well as transcend emotional barriers. Photos, art, humor, and poetry will also inspire your continuing action.**

**The design of *Choose Courage* echoes the dynamism of life. Like the blended, spontaneous nature of jazz, this interactive book uses a range of disciplines to support fresh ideas and menus of processes; weave them into what you want and need. Since the approach reflects the incremental nature of actual progress, take the small steps in whatever order makes sense to you. Or use the sequence offered. You'll be prompting your own potential and useful contributions from and to others.**

# THE CHOOSE COURAGE HANDBOOKS

      Promote your progress based on what engages and inspires you in Ruth's major book: Choose Courage: Step Into the Life You Want. For further encouragement, explore the four related handbooks below in addition to *Profit from Problems*. New formats to promote your happiness and joy are planned. Custom-designed for your enjoyment, adaptation, and action, all handbooks are about 50-100 pages and interactive. They also offer powerful processes for group training and development. Click on the handbook titles to purchase your copies!

Currently available handbooks:

| | |
|---|---|
| | Step Into the Success You Want: Sparking Your Powers (Choose Courage Handbook #1)<br>July 31, 2014<br>By Ruth Schimel, Ph.D.<br><br>Create success as you define it and reduce barriers to progress. |
| | Step Into the Success You Want: Building Bridges to Achievement (Choose Courage Handbook #2)<br>November 11, 2014<br>By Ruth Schimel, Ph.D.<br><br>Pursue your true interests, manage time, attract merited attention, discover your and others' heroes within, and access your wisdom. |
| | Choose Courage In Your Relationships: Empower Yourself First (Choose Courage Handbook #3)<br>March 29, 2015<br>By Ruth Schimel, Ph.D.<br><br>Make relationships flourish using your full range of interpersonal skills, viable expectations, care for others and unique charm. |

## Choose Courage in Your Relationships: Thrive Together
### (Choose Courage Handbook #4)
### November 19, 2015
### By Ruth Schimel, Ph.D.

Benefit from others' originality and strengths in partnerships, friendships, love, and intergenerational situations. Use these processes to improve your choices.

**Ruth M. Schimel, Ph.D.**

**Career & Life Management Consultant**

**202.659.1772**

www.ruthschimel.com    ruth@ruthschimel.com

**Use your good judgment, intuition, intellect, and common sense as you apply and adapt suggestions and guidance from this handbook.**

**Please do not use the text and illustrative material in this handbook for commercial purposes without written permission from the author. If used for academic purposes only, do not make any changes and notify the author in advance with details of use.**

Cover graphic by Blen Getahun, www.blengdesign.com

ISBN-13: 9780692682890 (Choose Courage Publishing)
ISBN-10: 0692682899

# LIMIT OF LIABILITY AND DISCLAIMER

# DEDICATION

This handbook is offered with appreciation to my clients and readers, as well as to my collaborator and production editor, Kathleen Sindell, Ph.D. (www.kathleensindell.com)

# TABLE OF CONTENTS

INTRODUCTION.................................................................................................................1

    KNOWLEDGE.................................................................................................3

    SKILLS.........................................................................................................4

    ABILITIES.....................................................................................................4

    NEXT STEPS................................................................................................5

REALITIES IN CHOICES AND RELATIONSHIPS.................................................................7

NEGOTIATE TO SOLVE PROBLEMS...................................................................................9

DEFINITIONS RELATED TO CONFLICT RESOLUTION.......................................................10

    CONFLICT: WHAT'S IT ALL ABOUT..............................................................10

    CHARACTERISTICS OF CONFLICT................................................................10

    CHARACTERISTICS OF LINGERING CONFLICT,.............................................11

    TYPES OF CONFLICT RESOLUTON...............................................................11

    VIOLENT....................................................................................................11

    PEACEFUL.................................................................................................11

    NEGOTIATION............................................................................................12

    AMBIVALENCE ABOUT CONFLICT:...............................................................12

BENEFITS AND RISKS OF CONFLICT RESOLUTION.........................................................13

CONVENTIONAL APPROACH TO NEGOTIATION.............................................................14

    ADVANTAGES OF POSITIONAL BARGAINING................................................14

    DISADVANTAGES OF POSITIONAL BARGAINING...........................................14

WIN-WIN APPROACH TO NEGOTIATION........................................................................15

    PEOPLE.....................................................................................................15

    INTERESTS................................................................................................15

    OPTIONS...................................................................................................15

    CRITERIA..................................................................................................15

STYLES OF NEGOTIATION..............................................................................................15

PROCESSES FOR NEGOTIATION.....................................................................................16

    STRENGTHENING YOUR READINESS FOR NEGOTIATION..............................18

    SOME GUIDELINES FOR PRACTICING NEGOTIATING SKILLS:........................19

OPPORTUNITIES IN CULTURAL DIFFERENCES ................................................. 20

CULTURAL EXPOSURE THROUGH A FILM ..................................................... 21

CULTURAL ISSUES IN LARGER CONTEXTS ................................................... 21

ENJOY CULTURAL VARIETY ....................................................................... 25

BENEFIT FROM DISCOMFORT IN DIFFERENCES ............................................ 26

THINK AGAINST YOURSELF TO THINK FOR YOURSELF ................................... 27

## GUIDE ONE: BENEFIT FROM THE BRAIN IN YOUR GUT ..................................... 29

PREPARATION ....................................................................................... 29

INGREDIENTS ....................................................................................... 30

LIKELY RESULTS OF YOUR EFFORTS ........................................................... 30

TRUST YOUR INTUITION .......................................................................... 30

FROM DISTRACTION TO FOCUS .................................................................. 31

FROM INTUITION TO ACTION .................................................................... 32

FOR ADDITIONAL INSIGHT, LEARNING, AND GUIDANCE ............................... 32

## GUIDE TWO: WAYS TO UNTANGLE PROBLEMS ............................................. 35

PREPARATION ....................................................................................... 36

INGREDIENTS ....................................................................................... 36

LIKELY RESULTS OF YOUR EFFORTS ........................................................... 36

OVERVIEW AND OPPORTUNITIES ............................................................. 36

PROBLEMS ARE NOT ALWAYS SOLVABLE .................................................... 37

FIRST, DESCRIBE THE PROBLEM ACCURATELY ............................................ 38

UNCOVER PROBLEM COMPLEXITY AND LAYERS .......................................... 40

NO ONE BEST WAY: PROCESSES TO CONSIDER ........................................... 41

GROUP BRAINSTORMING: FOCUSING AND FOLLOW-UP ............................... 42

CASE ANALYSIS APPROACH TO PROBLEM SOLVING ...................................... 43

CONVENTIONAL RESEARCH APPROACH ..................................................... 43

APPROACH FOR RESOURCE-BASED PROBLEMS ........................................... 44

GENERIC PROBLEM SOLVING ........................................................................ 44

CONCLUSIONS.......................................................................................... 45

FOR ADDITIONAL INSIGHT, LEARNING AND GUIDANCE.................................... 45

## GUIDE THREE: MANAGE RELATIONSHIP SABOTEURS ............................. 49

PREPARATION........................................................................................... 50

INGREDIENTS ........................................................................................... 50

LIKELY RESULTS OF YOUR EFFORTS ............................................................. 50

SITUATIONS THAT HARBOR SABOTEURS ........................................................ 50

MENU FOR MANAGING SABOTEURS.............................................................. 52

    DESCRIBE THE SITUATION .................................................................. 52
    MANAGE YOUR OWN LIMITING HABITS................................................... 52
    STRATEGIES FOR CONTINUING PROGRESS............................................... 53
    EXPRESS YOUR FEARS AND ANXIETIES TO YOURSELF FIRST........................ 53
    TAKE NOTES DURING EXCHANGES OR RIGHT AFTERWARD.......................... 55
    PREPARE TO HANDLE A RANGE OF OUTCOMES........................................ 56
    PREPARE FOR ACTUAL EXCHANGE WITH THE SABOTEUR. .......................... 56
    RE-ENERGIZE YOUR SENSE OF HUMOR .................................................. 56

FOR ADDITIONAL INSIGHT, LEARNING AND GUIDANCE.................................... 58

## GUIDE FOUR: TRANSCEND LIMITING SITUATIONS ............................. 59

PREPARATION........................................................................................... 59

INGREDIENTS ........................................................................................... 59

LIKELY RESULTS OF YOUR EFFORTS ............................................................. 60

SEEDS FOR PROGRESS IN CHALLENGES......................................................... 60

FOR ADDITIONAL INSIGHT, LEARNING AND GUIDANCE.................................... 67

## GUIDE FIVE: BLOCK THE BULLIES — WORK AND BEYOND .................. 69

PREPARATION........................................................................................... 69

INGREDIENTS ........................................................................................... 70

LIKELY RESULTS OF YOUR EFFORTS ............................................................. 70

THE BULLIES' SETUP ................................................................................. 70

FALLOUT FROM BULLYING .................................................................... 71

OPTIONS FOR DEALING WITH BULLIES NOW .................................... 72

DOCUMENT THE SITUATION ............................................................ 72

CONNECT WITH TRUSTWORTHY, SUPPORTIVE PEOPLE.................... 72

DEVELOP VIABLE, INDEPENDENT OPTIONS ...................................... 73

CONTINUING DANGERS AND OPPORTUNITIES.................................. 74

FOR ADDITIONAL INSIGHT, LEARNING, AND GUIDANCE ................... 77

GUIDE SIX: USE YOUR POWER — FULLY............................................. 79

PREPARATION................................................................................... 79

INGREDIENTS .................................................................................. 79

LIKELY RESULTS OF YOUR EFFORTS ................................................. 80

MEANINGS OF POWER ....................................................................80

FOR ADDITIONAL INSIGHT, LEARNING, AND GUIDANCE ................... 84

## APPENDICES

INDEX.............................................................................................. 86

APPENDIX A: DEFINITION OF COURAGE ........................................... 89

DEFINITION OF COURAGE ............................................................... 90

    Four Concepts Complementary to Courage.................................... 91

APPENDIX B: CYCLES OF COURAGE .................................................. 93

ABOUT THE AUTHOR ...................................................................... 97

# CHOOSE COURAGE
# IN YOUR RELATIONSHIPS:
# PROFIT FROM PROBLEMS

"Power resides in the moment of transition from a past to a new state."

~ Ralph Waldo Emerson, American essayist, lecturer, and poet ~

"Becoming courageous is a process that involves the willingness to realize your true capacities by going through discomfort, fear, anxiety, or suffering and taking wholehearted, responsible action."

~ Ruth M. Schimel, Ph.D., Career & Life Management Consultant ~

# INTRODUCTION

Problems and people tend to keep company. But since no person, situation — or even problem — rarely stays static, there's always hope for improvement and opportunities for effective action. Given these realities, this handbook is designed to help you profit from possibilities inherent in problems, issues, and blocks. Why let them limit your personal and professional relationships as well as quality of life, now and in the future?

Instead, create good outcomes for yourself using your experience, knowledge, and skills. As you bring them together with focused tools, leads, and insights from this handbook, you'll be even more effective in actual situations. Let the good will implicit in your values and interests infuse your communication and use of resources. All these processes can energize and inspire you to promote pleasure and progress over time.

Practical steps and guidance are available for you throughout this handbook. Let's start with your own interpersonal skills, especially since you may not appreciate them all nor see ways to strengthen and add to them. Why focus on yourself initially?

First, that's where you have more choices and influence. Starting within yourself also provides viable alternatives to blaming others over whom you likely have limited control. Your own powers will become more apparent as you specify your current capabilities using the self-assessment below. The five minutes you take to complete the first part will remind you of your strengths. Periodic reviews will support confidence for action and continuing progress. You may also see new ways to improve your skills, abilities, and knowledge.

Second, the assessment helps you identify new skills to learn and apply in order to strengthen the quality and quantity of your relationships. And, third, your thoughtful choices about when, how, where, why, and with whom to use your strengths will create additional advantages and opportunities.

Actually, the value of interpersonal skills starts earlier in life than you may think. For example, *The Washington Post* recently reported on data collected in Nashville, Seattle, rural Pennsylvania, and Durham, North Carolina schools since 1991. The outcome based on two decades of tracking 753 kindergarteners indicated their behaviors could predict later success related to getting a college degree and jobs. (See article: *If You Want Your Children to Succeed, Teach Them to Share in Kindergarten* by Emma Brown: http://wapo.st/1CJR5t6.)

Related to the "works and plays well with others" line I remember from my kindergarten report cards, here are the criteria used for assessment of children in the research:

- Resolves peer problems on his/her own.
- Is very good at understanding other people's feelings.
- Shares materials with others.
- Cooperates with peers without prompting.
- Is helpful to others.
- Listens to others' point of view.
- Can give suggestions and opinions without being bossy.
- Acts friendly toward others.

No doubt you'll note the parallels between these behaviors and the adult skills listed in the following self-assessment designed for your own situation and use.

## USE YOUR FULL INTERPERSONAL CAPACITIES

When you take five minutes right now to review your current levels of skills, knowledge, and abilities, you'll get an immediate sense of optimism about your interpersonal strengths. The information will help you see what you can do to contribute to your own effectiveness with other people in specific ways. You'll also be better able to assist them with their development.

When you feel adventuresome, share the assessment format below or even results with anyone you wish. For example, converse with trusted supervisors, colleagues, subordinates, friends, and family. Others may complete it for themselves and for discussion of mutual perceptions. In addition, use the process to identify interaction patterns, group learning opportunities, and issues to address.

On a scale of 1 to 5 (highest), highlight or circle the number that reflects your current level of expertise; if the description is not relevant, just ignore it. Alternatively, if it's a subject or process you want to check out, do a little online research. When not sure of where you stand numerically, always be generous with yourself.

In the spaces provided at the end of each of the three sections, add other capacities based on your ideas and those of people who know you in a variety of contexts. For insights and leads, pay special attention to the qualities you admire in others and to situations you tend to avoid or in which you feel uncomfortable.

### Knowledge

1 2 3 4 5   1. Group dynamics (interaction among participants)

1 2 3 4 5   2. Proxemics (how physical location in a group influences behavior)

1 2 3 4 5   3. Cultural and ethnic differences relevant to your situation

1 2 3 4 5   4. Types and uses of interpersonal skills assessments

1 2 3 4 5   5. Communication theory and processes

1 2 3 4 5   6. Own interpersonal issues

1 2 3 4 5   7. Nonverbal communication

1 2 3 4 5   8. Human relations theory and processes

1 2 3 4 5   9. _____

1 2 3 4 5   10. _____

**Skills**

1 2 3 4 5    11. Giving feedback

1 2 3 4 5    12. Interviewing and other ways to gather information from others

1 2 3 4 5    13. Listening for what's not literal in what people say

1 2 3 4 5    14. Analyzing an interpersonal situation or issue

1 2 3 4 5    15. Synthesizing information about an interpersonal problem

1 2 3 4 5    16. Naming specific emotions and feelings in yourself

1 2 3 4 5    17. Identifying specific emotions and feelings in others

1 2 3 4 5    18. Leading an interpersonal skill development process

1 2 3 4 5    19. Being alert to nonverbal cues you give others

1 2 3 4 5    20. Reading nonverbal cues in others

1 2 3 4 5    21. Identifying reasons for and types of conflict

1 2 3 4 5    22. Diagnosing reasons for ineffective communication

1 2 3 4 5    23. Using metaphors and other ways to enrich what you say

1 2 3 4 5    24. _____

1 2 3 4 5    25. _____


**Abilities**

1 2 3 4 5    26. Appreciating and understanding human diversity

1 2 3 4 5    27. Intuition

1 2 3 4 5    28. Sense of humor about your foibles, perceptions, and ambitions

1 2 3 4 5    29. Good judgment about when to seek assistance and feedback

1 2 3 4 5    30. Willingness to consider unsolicited feedback

1 2 3 4 5    31. Capacity to hear the actual message behind what is being said

1 2 3 4 5   32. Ability to inspire trust

1 2 3 4 5   33. Self-confidence based on reality

1 2 3 4 5   34. Facilitation of meetings

1 2 3 4 5   35. Effective participation in and contributions to groups

1 2 3 4 5   36. Empathy: ability to imagine, or understand others' feelings

1 2 3 4 5   37. Capacity to serve audiences and read reactions while speaking

1 2 3 4 5   38. _____

1 2 3 4 5   39. _____

### Next Steps

1. Review your strengths (any capacity you labeled 4 or 5). Perhaps group them to determine patterns related to self-presentation, information gathering, and understanding how your behavior can influence others. Certainly mention and celebrate the strengths you note below.

_____

_____

_____

_____

_____

2. For every 1, 2, or 3 you have circled above, consider whether or not you want or need to develop that capacity further. Look for patterns among the ones you have chosen to identify key areas for strengthening. Mention them here.

_____

_____

3. Now, choose one or two areas (particular skills, abilities, or knowledge) to develop or strengthen, specifying a few, manageable objectives for each.

_____

_____

_____

4. For anything you want to improve that is identified in (3) above, circle methods to use from the list and others you add below.

- peer collaboration
- workshops, courses, and online classes (MOOCs)
- verbal, written, and audio-visual feedback
- mentors
- books, articles, guides, and online resources
- observation of others in real and reel life
- self-study program or process
- teach and train others
- _____
- _____

5. Create a simple plan for follow through with your first choice, possibly including:

- your learning strategy for your first choice
- some specific criteria for evaluating progress
- who will help or collaborate with you
- what you would enjoy doing to acknowledge and reward your progress

6. As you wish, repeat steps 2 - 5 for other capacities you want to strengthen or develop.

Since continuing improvement of interpersonal capacities is often best nurtured in interaction with others, find a partner or form a small group of about four to five people who would like to work together. Assessing and developing your interpersonal capacities in a vacuum can be sterile and less productive, however uncomfortable you may feel when you first give and get feedback.

To promote productive exchange, you'll be better motivated and enriched when collaborators have something different, unique, or complementary to offer. In fact, that's a good way to start the conversation. Focus on capacities each of you brings to the process even before you set some simple guidelines for learning, practice, and mutual feedback. Then you can discuss and decide on what you want to do to honor everyone's needs, interests, and time.

# REALITIES IN CHOICES AND RELATIONSHIPS

You've already started well to address problems, issues, and blocks by appreciating your capacities and potential via the assessment, perhaps in more detail than usual. Yet, since this handbook is about relationships which involve a variety of people, your insights and actions can only go so far. That's why tools, ideas, and inspiration are offered to encourage continuing use and development of your strengths and conscious choices of how to influence others. Ultimately, your willingness to understand and address the interaction and natural complexity in your relationships can benefit everyone.

Nevertheless, the very nature of your changing environment and dynamic tendencies of other people may inhibit your best efforts. You'll continue to encounter behavioral filters of privilege related to racial, economic, and social advantages. That's even expressed in neural activity related to social pecking orders as discussed by Robert Sapolsky about how higher status people tend to attract greater attention. See the research on this in his 2015 *Wall Street Journal* article, *Brain Reflexes That Monitor the Pecking Order* http://on.wsj.com/1TBOzse.

On the other hand, lack of opportunity for some people also affects relationships as you've no doubt experienced or noticed. In many instances, culture is a crucial foundation that complicates as well as provides depth and interest. (See discussion of cultural matters and possibilities they offer at the end of this Introduction.)

Furthermore, each individual's behavior is influenced by genes and epigenetics, or how environment and experience affect the chemistry of DNA. In other words, the interaction between nature and nurture does not tell the whole story, as current research has found. For example, genes themselves can be affected by stressful events such as abuse, violence, or illness. And variations in particular genes predispose children to different reactions as discussed in Alison Gopnik's *Wall Street Journal* article: *Aggression in Children Makes Sense - Sometimes*, http://on.wjs.com/1oqut28.

In fact, imposed situations can shift actions of some people. Over forty years ago, the research of Stanley Milgram showed how unquestioning obedience to authority led to hurtful behavior. About the same time, Philip Zimbardo did somewhat related research on the psychology of imprisonment and how the power of total control could distort behavior of guards. Based on that inquiry, Zimbardo believes most everyone can be evil.

That both professors used male college students in their experiments may have affected results, in my opinion. The students were young, perhaps hormonally flush and more easily influenced by authority. To make up your own mind, though, see *The Stanford Prison Experiment* film and an earlier related documentary, *Quiet Rage*.

As you know from your own life, everyday professional and personal situations that do not involve laboratory or experimental situations naturally include relationships that are challenging and variable, no matter the level of caring. Marriages and other partnerships of months and years have frustrations and dark times. Among many, issues may involve money, sex, children, health, doubts, and confusion — not to mention, ironically, conflict avoidance. These realities are not helped by expectations of continuing honeymoons and consistent experiences and behaviors. Yet even continuously pleasant times may lose appeal; such predictability may bring a sense of security that eventually becomes boring due to lack of variety and surprises.

Work situations are also in flux as the cast of characters, internal resources, and the economy affect power relationships and content. Comfort in continuity or predictability some people prefer is therefore difficult to sustain. As mastery and a sense of control is reached, repetition may also lead to boredom and atrophy. Except perhaps for initial learning, routines can lead to "tennis elbow" of the mind or an itch for change. Since the learning curve is thought by some to be five to seven years, you can expect that preparing for change will serve your interests and keep relationships — not to mention your own life — vibrant, stimulating, and healthy.

In *Exit, Voice, and Loyalty,* political economist Albert O. Hirschman provided ways to prepare for and deal with flux in personal and professional relationships. Although his study related to responses to the decline of firms, organizations, and states, Hirschman's ideas are also relevant to personal and professional relationships. Using his title as a guide for choices and action, gird yourself to leave when necessary, speak up to protect your interests and move to a healthier place, or accept realities and stay put with grace.

Considering all these possibilities, resolving conflicts with others is another skill to strengthen or add to your repertoire. Following is a range of choices to improve your capacities for managing personal as well as professional situations. Take what's useful, make it your own, and leave the rest.

# NEGOTIATE TO SOLVE PROBLEMS

As promised in the second handbook on relationships, *Thrive Together*, this Introduction includes more specific guidance on negotiation (see definition under types of conflict resolution later on). It is one of the more effective processes and tools for finding common ground in conflicts as well as to transcend blocks, issues, and problems. While not a magical solution, the negotiation process will help you move forward in your relationships, at home and work, and in community. Consider and experiment with whatever ideas and steps below expand your repertoire and suit you, taking action that relates to your needs, situation, and goals.

To appreciate your own attitudes, ambivalence, and assumptions, you may find it useful to jot down now some keywords about what conflict means to you by answering the following questions. Those responses will help you understand how you tend to deal with conflict in various ways, for better, for worse, or somewhere in between.

- What main words and phrases do you associate with conflict?

_____

_____

_____

- Name a few significant experiences that influenced your attitude toward conflict.

_____

_____

_____

- What one or two patterns have you noticed in how you address conflict and/or avoid useful action related to conflict?

_____

_____

_____

Based on your answers to any of these questions, how would you describe below your readiness to address a conflict, or possibly misunderstanding that sabotages or limits a current, important relationship? For example, are you curious, averse, interested, or committed? What steps are you willing to take? (Subsequent information on conflict resolution and negotiation may help you clarify your responses. But noting them below as well, could provide your more current, authentic views, unaffected by that following information.)

_____

_____

_____

# DEFINITIONS RELATED TO CONFLICT RESOLUTION

The following information and ideas are based on summarizing and integrating approaches by experts and practitioners. Use critical thinking and common sense to apply them to your situations. You may also want to explore them with a range of people you respect who are familiar with you and realities you face. (FYI: Much of this was part of conflict resolution course material I put together for teaching at universities as well as experience volunteering as a community mediator for several years and during diplomatic work.)

### CONFLICT: WHAT'S IT ALL ABOUT

Conflict is an event or process that reflects perceived or actual differences among individuals, groups, or organizations. It can relate to past, current, or future situations as well as to a variety of stakeholders who have issues, goals, and interests that vary or do not connect well.

Use the following descriptions of various characteristics of conflict and lingering conflict for diagnosis of your situations. Check what applies, restating any to reflect what you face. Insights from reviewing those choices may help you identify opportunities for amelioration and action.

### *Characteristics of conflict* can include:

- Goals are uncertain or changing.
- Communication is more confusing than usual.
- Values are explicitly or implicitly at odds.

- Emotions are involved and affect perception and understanding — information can therefore be distorted or misinterpreted.
- Threats are made or implied.
- Money or some material prize is often an option for action, cure, or symbol of settlement.
- Time is typically an element and may be a motivator.
- Desire to settle is usually present, but other factors such as retribution and resentment may distort or distract from progress.
- Most everything is negotiable (when addressed with open minds and creativity).
- Resolution can be an outcome, including forgiveness, exchange of goods and/or services, changes in expectations, and commitment to an improved situation.

*Characteristics of lingering conflict,* with implied opportunities for amelioration, are:

- Goals of parties are not clearly established.
- Costs of maintaining conflict are not entirely apparent or assessed by parties.
- Benefits of settlement are not well-articulated and weighed.
- Each side is hooked into need to punish the other one.
- One or both sides think another person or process will resolve the conflict to their advantage.
- There is no or limited willingness to question or discuss positions and possibilities.
- Trust is weak or not well-established.
- Influencers and others with power are stubborn, ego-bound, or stuck in self-righteousness.
- Collusive sub-groups or individuals are saboteurs.

## TYPES OF CONFLICT RESOLUTON ARE:

*Violent*: terrorism, guerilla warfare, conventional war, riots, murder, imposition of one set of interests on another, hostage-taking

*Peaceful*: bypass people, units or organizations; make alliances to bring pressure; lie; withhold information; leave (transfer, promotion, resign); negotiate, mediate, litigate; develop policies and programs with input, commitment, and agreement from all stakeholders; vote

***Negotiation*** is a peaceful means of conflict resolution which occurs when two or more parties work out actual, perceived, or potential differences. Applying to cooperative, neutral, and adversarial relationships, it includes:

- opportunities to exchange promises
- ways to check compliance
- constructive outcomes that benefit all parties
- ways for parties to retain power they value

**AMBIVALENCE ABOUT CONFLICT:** The dictionary has a range of definitions which may explain many people's ambivalence toward conflict. They are:

- open fighting, warfare
- disagreement or disharmony, a clash
- (from psychology) the opposition or simultaneous functioning of mutually exclusive desires, impulses, or tendencies
- collision

No wonder so many people prefer to avoid dealing with conflict. Discomfort, ambiguity, and possible loss seem associated with the word, if not also present in actual experiences. The void of unknown outcomes hovers. Often, the worst outcome is imagined, certainly making the process of becoming courageous relevant!

Yet, consider conflicts in your life or those you have observed that have been worked out in fair ways. When has the risk, or at least an honest try, been worth the effort? In retrospect, how might you or others have proceeded more effectively? Mention a few ways below:

_____

_____

_____

Figuring out the value and risk of addressing conflict in your personal and professional life is challenging. To make an honest effort, list below the main potential benefits and likely outcomes from addressing one significant interpersonal conflict you have in mind. Then mention a few likely probabilities that could result if you don't deal with it.

_____

_____

_____

_____

# BENEFITS AND RISKS OF CONFLICT RESOLUTION

Following are many of the benefits from using your skills in conflict resolution to work out differences. You are likely to:

- Save time by getting to the point through focusing and addressing issues.
- Use tangible resources more effectively.
- Improve understanding of different viewpoints as a basis for better planning and action.
- Encourage commitment of all parties to an agreed-upon goal.
- Feel more at ease or at least relieved of main tensions.
- Encounter new ideas and opportunities.
- Strengthen trust to support current and future cooperation and collaboration.
- Enjoy and deepen professional and personal relationships.
- Meet goals and objectives.

What other benefits would you add?

_____

_____

Risks may include:

- Time is lost in efforts to resolve conflict.
- Vulnerabilities become more apparent and intrusive.
- Disappointment and loss of commitment occur when efforts do not pan out.
- Problem or issue possibly escalates due to misunderstanding, ineptitude, or sabotage.
- Stalemate occurs and sour feelings linger.

What other risks would you add?

The following summary information reflects what many professionals say about the process of conflict resolution through negotiation. Use and adapt it to enrich your repertoire as you practice the art.

# CONVENTIONAL APPROACH TO NEGOTIATION

The conventional approach to negotiation is often labeled positional bargaining. In this process, each side:

- takes a position

- argues for its position

- makes concessions to reach compromise

*Advantages of positional bargaining* are:

- Each side tells the other what it wants.

- An anchor is provided in a difficult situation because parties use a predictable process.

- The process may lead to acceptable agreement.

*Disadvantages of positional bargaining* are:

- possible inflexibility of positions

- attention to positions rather than to underlying concerns of parties and collaborative, creative possibilities

- splitting of differences between parties rather than development of carefully-designed solutions that benefit both sides

- possible inefficiency — the more extreme the positions, the smaller the concessions

- tendency to succumb to contest of wills, egos

# WIN-WIN APPROACH TO NEGOTIATION

This approach pays attention to both the substance and process of negotiation by focusing on the merits or opportunities in the conflict. It recognizes that no side benefits when one party is hurt by the agreement and the relationship continues; the disadvantaged party then has little motivation to honor the terms and may even seek retribution. Furthermore, it assumes that parties working collaboratively, in good faith, can develop creative and useful ideas that will result in a better arrangement than merely making concessions. This is often called a win-win outcome. (From *Getting to Yes* by Fisher and Ury and *Getting Together* by Fisher and Brown.)

Following are basic tenets of this approach adapted from *Getting to Yes*:

**People**: Identify and clarify personality conflicts and emotions or feelings that affect communication and trust, treating them separately.

**Interests**: Address the human needs of the negotiators by identifying each side's requirements, desires, concerns, and fears.

**Options**: Invent together alternatives for mutual gain.

**Criteria**: Develop agreed-upon, useful criteria for judging merits of agreement such as market value, precedent, scientific judgment, professional standards, efficiency, costs, tradition, reciprocity, equal treatment, time, effectiveness, fairness, etc. Then determine together:

- Is agreement efficient and viable?

- Does agreement improve or avoid damage to the relationship?

- When agreement is possible, is it wise?

- How does the agreement benefit most everyone's long-term interests, support basic goals, and encourage possible cooperation or collaboration of the parties?

# STYLES OF NEGOTIATION

The descriptions of five negotiating styles below are adapted from the Thomas-Kilmann Conflict Mode Instrument which can be accessed and purchased through search engines such as Google. Use your own experience and insight to modify and/or add to them. As negotiations proceed, identify individuals' styles or a similar version; maybe develop your own definitions. Based on these insights, choose appropriate strategies to improve communication and meet objectives of the parties.

In some instances, styles may be so contradictory that negotiation will be thwarted (e.g. competing and avoiding). If you come to this conclusion, you may want to consider alternatives to negotiating on your own such as leaving the situation, reconsidering your degree of commitment, or third-party intervention.

| | |
|---|---|
| **Competing** | "I'm going to win this one." (and you'll lose) |
| **Avoiding** | "I don't want to talk about it." (delay at all costs) |
| **Compromising** | "I'm going to give in order to get." (we'll find some middle ground) |
| **Accommodating** | "Whatever you want...." (I yield) |
| **Collaborating** | "Let's work together to find a mutually beneficial outcome." |

# PROCESSES FOR NEGOTIATION

In many actual situations, you'll rarely have the luxury, need, or even interest in following the step-by-step processes provided below. When available, information is likely to be developed more informally, perhaps in different sequence. Time may be limited. Intuition and sometimes impatience may influence behavior rather than just the rationality and logic of these guidelines. Saboteurs might want to derail the process, requiring more assertive, strategic leadership and management.

Nevertheless, the following can be a useful checklist. Adapt it for structuring your thinking, strategy, and action as well as to ensure you use available resources and options. At the same time, be prepared to also proceed organically by taking advantage of what flows naturally and usefully.

- Be clear to yourself about your own objectives, perceptions, emotions, interests, and concerns.

- Learn as much about the situation as possible beforehand through analysis and conversation with a range of people.

- Discuss your view of options with others for their ideas and perspectives. When appropriate, keep them informed of progress.

- Obtain information related to the other side. That can include biographical data, finances, and public statements. Clarify your understanding of one another's goals, strategies, and values, preferably in conversation. The more open the communication, the greater likelihood of building trust.

- Identify common interests or at least overlapping concerns.

- Imagine what the other side truly wants and needs as well as their style of negotiating and sensitive buttons. Consider how your own tendencies will mesh and what you can do to create better communication, find common ground, and agree on outcomes.

- Develop an authentic negotiating approach for yourself, including a range of options. Visualize yourself in the negotiation, imagining how you would handle important contingencies.

- Keep evaluating your own assumptions based on what you sense, feel, and hear.

- Ask yourself what you don't yet know that would be useful to learn. If you can't obtain the information beforehand, how can you elicit it during the negotiation and informal conversations?

- Identify and organize information the other side needs to know to help them understand your perspective.

- Prepare several hypothetical situations to educate the other side to your point of view.

- Design, arrange, and provide the most fair, effective physical arrangements for the negotiation process and participants.

- Think of several appropriate ways to ease tensions such as telling a story on yourself or a joke that does not annoy or antagonize.

- Define and work toward your best alternative to a negotiated settlement (BATNA from *Getting to Yes*).

**Strengthening Your Readiness for Negotiation.** After reading and considering the foregoing, are you ready to use and adapt some of the ideas in a situation you are facing? Whether or not you are, now is the time to appreciate the skills and experience you already have with conflict resolution, based on what you have just read and know. That can remind you of how well-prepared you are to move forward effectively.

Use the suggested list below to review your strengths and readiness. Add other skills, abilities, and experience that relate to your situation in the spaces at the end. Circle the level that describes your current expertise: (1) is lowest and (5) is highest. Always be generous with your numerical choices.

When you've circled 1, 2, or 3, decide if you want to improve that capacity. If so, consider training, observing, reading, participating in workshops and courses, mentoring, on-the-job experience, and other methods you know about or can identify with some research.

1  2  3  4  5   Listening skills

1  2  3  4  5   Sense of humor about your situation and others' behavior

1  2  3  4  5   Analytical skills

1  2  3  4  5   Charm

1  2  3  4  5   Integrity

1  2  3  4  5   Synthesizing skills

1  2  3  4  5   Interpersonal skills

1  2  3  4  5   Awareness of others' nonverbal communication

1  2  3  4  5   Awareness of your own nonverbal communication

1  2  3  4  5   Willingness to let go of control that could limit good outcomes

1  2  3  4  5   Empathy: capacity to identify with others' feelings and needs

1  2  3  4  5   Evaluation of complex situations

1  2  3  4  5   Articulateness: ease and effectiveness of communication

1 2 3 4 5   Willingness to learn, stay open to new information and ideas

1 2 3 4 5   Experience with and interest in building trust

1 2 3 4 5   Clarity about goals

1 2 3 4 5   Intuition/gut feeling

1 2 3 4 5   Ability to deal with and make use of ambiguity

1 2 3 4 5   Patience

1 2 3 4 5   Creativity

1 2 3 4 5   Self-awareness and willingness to self-adjust

1 2 3 4 5   _____

1 2 3 4 5   _____

1 2 3 4 5   _____

## Some Guidelines for Practicing Negotiating Skills:

- Launch new skills as strongly as possible, starting with low-risk situations in which practicing will be more comfortable.
- Never let an exception occur until skills are strongly rooted.
- Seize the first, appropriate opportunity to use your skills.

To get started using your negotiating skills, briefly answer in a few words any of the following that will assist your progress:

- When and for what will you use your negotiation skills?

_____
_____

- What main impediments do you anticipate and what will you do about them?

_____
_____
_____

- What can you do to encourage others to learn more about the negotiation process so you all can work better together?

_____

_____

- How will you assess and reward your own and others' progress?

_____

_____

- Who will you enlist to assist you and other negotiators?

_____

_____

   **Now, what is your first step to resolve a conflict that is important to you? Briefly describe it below and block necessary time on your calendar for follow through on this and your other choices for action.**

_____

_____

_____

# OPPORTUNITIES IN CULTURAL DIFFERENCES

   Among significant influences on your relationships and conflict resolution opportunities you may not have explored fully are cultural differences. Attention to their variety and value can benefit most everyone involved. Even when there seem to be common experiences, geographic, familial, and individual variations are worth attention. Consider such aspects for strengthening and improving connections as well as for making progress with issues and conflicts.

   This general definition of culture itself exposes its power and influence on relationships. Culture is "the totality of socially transmitted behavior patterns, arts, beliefs, institutions and all other products of human work and thoughts characteristic of a community or population." As such, culture relates to a significant range of human activity.

Since culture is so all inclusive, it affects identity profoundly. Maybe that's why many people cling to their own, consciously and unconsciously. Some feel theirs is superior and that, by definition, others' cultures are inferior. Such attitudes may be protections from underlying fears and anxieties or just reflect limited connections with different people and situations. Unexpected benefits then can emerge through exposure, exploration, and experience.

For example, William Deresiewicz mentions in a book review of *The Great Wave* on the opening of Japan in the 19th century that "...there is no self-knowledge — and thus, in a sense, no true knowledge at all — without displacement." In other words, awareness and growth can bloom from the discomfort that often goes with exploring differences and experiencing being a stranger.

## CULTURAL EXPOSURE THROUGH A FILM

A variety of western European students demonstrated this process of growth through exposure to cultural differences in the French film *L'Auberge Espagnole* set in Barcelona, Spain. Their predictable conflicts about keeping things tidy in their shared apartment were less important than the real and important drama centered in relationships. Through exposure to one another and dealing with conflict, the students transcended stereotypes related to gender, language, and nationality.

The supposedly rigid German, constrained Brit, proper Frenchman and unfeminine lesbian revealed the appealing and complex individuals they actually were. What also emerged through the protagonist's efforts to find himself was the underlying human need for clarifying identity and direction for the future — a universal struggle of youth in a variety of cultures that often continues lifelong. (See the forthcoming section for additional ideas for learning about culture through the arts: Enjoy Cultural Variety.)

## CULTURAL ISSUES IN LARGER CONTEXTS

The apartment life in the *L'Auberge Espagnole* film is a microcosm of the characters' countries which are sometimes considered melting pots, possibly a romantic illusion of integration. Exploration of the history of nations actually reveals their patchworks of territories combining a variety of cultural groups that periodically struggle for control, influence, resources, and land. The obvious and underlying conflicts within and between countries are heightened by differences of race, religion, and class, occasionally overlaid with tribal issues. In fact, the Latin derivation of the word nation is tribe.

Despite the rich heterogeneity of the United States there is a wide range of issues reflecting cultural differences and values that show up as segregated enclaves. They affect almost everyone, directly or indirectly in relationships, neighborhoods, work, schools, friendships, travel as well as in prison populations.

Cultural conflicts continue as recent statistics reported in *The Wall Street Journal* show; there have been over 1000 anti-Jewish and half as many anti-Muslim hate crimes. Unfortunately, the latter figures, along with other acts of discrimination are increasing as the Middle East conflict continues to erupt beyond its borders. Reported infiltrations of extremists and criminals increasingly stoke fear and anxiety in the U.S.

September 11 shocked Americans into acknowledging their vulnerability to threats from abroad often related to political, religious, and ethnic differences. Even today, in a 2015 *New York Times* survey by its research and analytics department among 3,244 subscribers who chose to participate, 49% were afraid there will be another attack in their lifetime on the order of September 11. 29% said they did not expect one and 22% said they were not sure. This study occurred before the burgeoning of ISIS, aka ISIL or more appropriately DAIISH, and al Qaeda terrorism into Europe and Africa in 2015.

Sometimes related to cultural differences, the specter of domestic violence and terrorism, hovers as well. Whether they have proven mental illness or not, many perpetrators attack defenseless victims in everyday situations such as military recruiting facilities and movie theaters. The Oklahoma City bombing and Waco, Texas Branch Davidian siege are less recent examples of the centuries-long history of conflicts among ethnic, religious, cultural, and class groups in the United States. Many reflect overarching and aggravating issues such as poverty, urban decay, natural resource depletion and degradation, and weapons proliferation. Within such issues often reside simmering conflicts, reflecting differing cultural values, fears, and histories, not to mention power and ideological struggles.

Despite such disturbing and often destructive realities, many people still need and benefit from connecting with one another, whether they admit it or not. Without a modicum of peace and prosperity, almost everyone loses, whether they are "haves" or "have-nots." Then how to "just get along," how to foster understanding, acceptance, and even collaboration for mutual benefit?

There is potential for better understanding and acceptance in the following shifts and pressures which may stimulate mutual understanding and cooperation, perhaps even empathy.

- trends toward merging of members of different races, religions, and genders into family units
- relative increases in numbers and influence of people with different skin colors and ethnic backgrounds
- increased recognition by individuals, groups, and influencers of need to modify policies and devote resources to domestic issues such as mental illness, incarceration rates, and addictions leading to increased deaths from alcoholism, opioids, and heroin
- general matters such as aging, class structures, health, affordable housing, and education that relate to sustaining quality of life, economic viability, and public safety; they all have cultural aspects which complicate and potentially enrich situations and could forge a sense of community in some instances. An example is the aging in place Village movement throughout the U.S.
- international issues such as trade, refugees, nuclear proliferation, climate change, pollution, epidemics, cyberwarfare and many other matters that borders don't thwart affect individuals' lives

In today's world, no human being is an island, but neither is any country, ethnic group, religion, class, race, or gender. Although some with greater resources and perhaps fear can put gates around themselves, ultimately many will still be vulnerable to economic downturns, crime, terrorism, and epidemics. Change, for better and worse, cannot be stopped. But it may be influenced for the better by you as an individual and by collaborating with others through your range of relationships. In addition, your resources can include money and time as well as experience, education, leadership, and common sense. Continuing learning and caring about others can ease the transitions for everyone..

One way that will benefit most people at almost no cost is to learn about and appreciate cultural differences: what you want to embrace and modify in your own and what is valuable, possibly threatening, and enriching in others. This is a process available to anyone curious about what other people offer and aware of dangers in not understanding different and possibly conflicting motivations and values.

For example, how do you relate to these American cultural values shared by many in the U.S. and beyond?

- primacy of the individual
- action over contemplation
- competition as a major motivator in economic activity

For another view of American cultural values, you may be interested in this 2015 take on the mythology of American exceptionalism in *Bloomberg Business News*. See the five related charts from Jeremy Grantham: http://bloom.bg/1OTTQw7

There is nothing intrinsically right or wrong with these or many other cultural values. However, staying at one end of the spectrum at the expense of learning about and possibly integrating the advantages of alternatives may lead to a limiting rigidity. Instead, imagine what would happen if there were a range of ways to:

- identify, develop, and define the worth of individuals and groups
- gather, evaluate, and share information for mutual benefit and action
- be successful

Learning how other cultures and countries address such matters provides new ideas and possibilities. In Ireland, for example, a student prize recognizes generosity of spirit.

To increase flexibility within the United States, people could explore the realities of nonlinear processes or how things unfold. That understanding can contribute to making sense of complexity and paradox as well. In turn, such an approach provides ways to avoid boxing life's messiness into mere logic and analysis. In other words, dealing with seeming illogic can be an important basis for appreciating many important situations and behaviors.

Seeing what emerges from using analysis and synthesis together can be more powerful than simply seeking cause and effect relationships which don't reflect complex realities. There are often just too many variables and influences to assume one cause or action leads to one effect. As in relationships, both distractions and advantages occur in dynamic interactions. Emotions naturally add to the complexity as well as clarify direction for what may seem obscure.

To play with specific examples, consider other criteria for success beyond money, higher education, position, or power. One example could be satisfying relationships in which all parties benefit and grow. How would that definition of success influence your choices and behavior? No doubt you can think of other questions and approaches to spark your imagination and expand or deepen what you do and how you live.

As you appreciate the riches and possibilities in differences, see what opportunities emerge to improve your situation. What beneficial ways are there to support and learn from one another? What would happen when you explore other cultures with openness and curiosity?

This process may also expand thinking and pleasures as well as decrease disdain and fear of differences. Just as studying how individuals struggle through difficulties to become stronger, other cultures can provide good drawing boards for understanding, conversing, and finding alternatives to transcend problems. New opportunities and variety are possible, offsetting the boredom and stasis that often come with what's known and seemingly predictable.

# ENJOY CULTURAL VARIETY

Appreciating cultural differences does not mean giving up or limiting your own beliefs, nature, or way of living. But it can stimulate, educate, and entertain with new ideas and choices. The process also helps you confirm what you like and prefer about your own situation.

For adventure and pleasure, try any of the following ways to enrich, enlarge, and deepen your life by exploring others' beliefs and behaviors. To encourage your momentum, choose or adapt one for follow up within the next week or so.

**Learn about another culture** that intrigues you, within or outside this nation; imagine your own from its perspective.

**Study how an interesting culture evolved**, comparing and contrasting its history, and possibly its arts, with your own. Look for the commonalities and differences.

**Listen to and watch people from different cultures**. Engage them in conversation, asking questions and offering information about yourself, your ways of living, and customs, as appropriate.

**Identify how your own culture has affected your main values and actions**, for better and worse.

**Read biographies, autobiographies, and articles about people from different backgrounds** you find interesting or even challenging.

**Choose any examples from literature, dance, music, visual arts, theater, and film that seem new and engaging to you.** How does your experience with it relate to what you know about already and your expectations?

**Explore different foods and eating preferences** within and outside the United States. Prepare a meal with someone from another culture, sharing some favorite dishes.

Mention below your preferred choice or adaptation from the foregoing suggestions and specific steps (how, when, where, and with whom) for follow through.

_____

_____

_____

## BENEFIT FROM DISCOMFORT IN DIFFERENCES

Choosing what's comfortable and predictable can limit worthwhile challenges and opportunities. For example, a well-educated, sophisticated woman might prefer a doctor with a similar background in contrast to one from a different country or race with better credentials and patient ratings. If you have such tendencies, being aware of them can prepare you for making more conscious, effective choices.

In a possibly less benevolent situation, imagine walking down a street and noticing a rowdy group of teenagers from another race or ethnic group walking toward you. Do you make way for them, cross the street, keep barreling ahead with eyes averted, or look them in their eyes? That decision is best made when you know something about their values and tendencies to help you predict what could happen and how to stay safe in a specific context.

You may be interested in knowing about 2015 research on anxiety in the United States. It notes that we are distinctive in our emphasis on feelings, though some inarticulateness or avoidance of dealing with them I've noticed makes me wonder about this generalization. For the full discussion, see *The New York Times* article, *The Anxious Americans,* by Stanford University anthropology professor T. M. Luhrmann at http://tinyurl.com/pbl8juf.

On a more general level, address any unspecified anxiety you feel about terrorist threats by taking reasonable precautions based on understanding the values and behaviors of such people. Though fear of a specific source may not disappear, learning what's behind their actions may help dissipate the anxiety expressed in a sense of impotency and doom that comes from hearing about vague and continuing dangers. Your knowledge and insight can also help you make effective decisions related to travel, work, family activities, and other aspects of your life, as well as local and national policies. For a discussion of religious violence, see Rabbi Jonathan Sacks' 2015 book: *Not in God's Name: Confronting Religious Violence*.

# THINK AGAINST YOURSELF TO THINK FOR YOURSELF

Although I'm not a fan of French existentialist philosopher Jean Paul Sartre, I can still learn from the way he embraced differences. Sartre explained why he wanted to study one of his own countrymen, the writer Gustave Flaubert, with whom he had little in common: "Because he is the opposite of what I am. I need to rub against something that puts me into question. In *The Words* I wrote, 'I have often thought against myself.' That sentence has never been understood... But, in fact, that's exactly how one should think: One should always be questioning one's own assumptions." Thinking against yourself will not only enrich your life, but also protect it; understanding another perspective can help you prepare for and engage with the unknown, whether it's appealing or threatening.

To think for as well as against yourself for your own benefit and to profit from problems, this handbook also provides you with the six guides below. As always, adjust the ideas and suggestions to your nature and situation. The guides are designed to be flexible, to honor differences in readers and users. Experiment with relevant applications that inspire you and relate usefully to your situation in order to improve your relationships, take good care of yourself, and move forward.

*Guide One: Benefit from the Brain in Your*

*Guide Two: Ways to Untangle Problems*

*Guide Three: Manage Relationship Saboteurs*

*Guide Four: Transcend Limiting Situations*

*Guide Five: Block the Bullies: At Work and Guide*

*Guide Six: Use Your Power — Fully*

Perhaps this quote from a father of modern aviation, Wilbur Wright, will contribute to your progress: *No bird soars in a calm.*

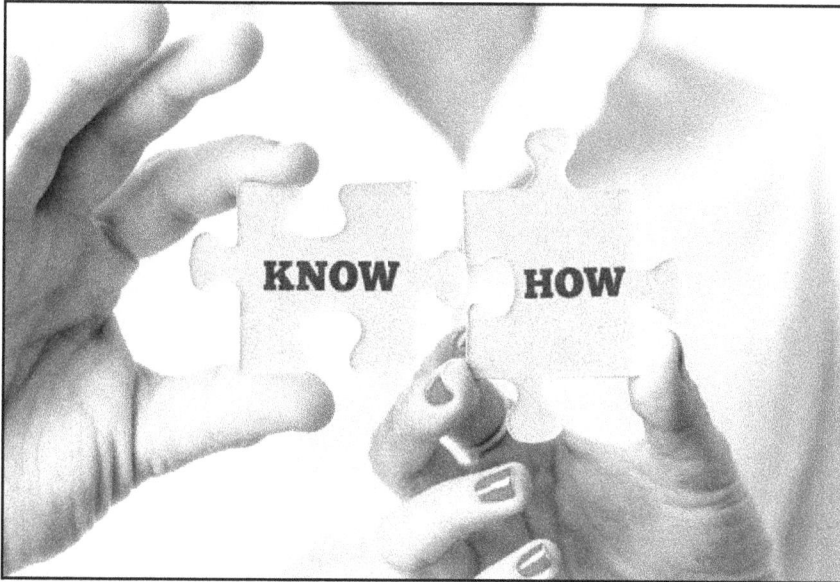

*You'll have know-how in hand when you integrate your gut feeling with what your brain tells you.*

## GUIDE ONE: BENEFIT FROM THE BRAIN IN YOUR GUT

*"Trust yourself. You know more than you think you do."*

·· Benjamin Spock, pediatrician and author ·-

## PREPARATION

Five minutes to read and choose a situation to use all your smarts

# INGREDIENTS

Having faith in your intuition

Appreciating mind-body connections

Integrating reason and emotion

# LIKELY RESULTS OF YOUR EFFORTS

Avoidance of mistakes and detours

Greater confidence in choices

Successes from your insights

Well-founded relationships

## TRUST YOUR INTUITION

I sense you know that gut feeling. Some call it intuition. What has happened to you when you've ignored or dismissed it?

If you sometimes regret ignoring your intuition, that's one good reason to heed the messages you receive from your gut. Another is even more promising: the neurotransmitters in your brain are the same class of chemicals that carry information among the neurons in your intestines. That process contributes to your imagining, thinking, and creating; it also helps you store information. In fact, next to those in your brain, the second greatest number of neurotransmitters in your body is in your gut.

Perhaps intuitive information is ignored or dismissed because it doesn't seem to come from your own intellect or someone else's knowledge you can confirm. Intuition doesn't seem to count because you don't know its source. But actually that source is within you, accrued over time. So remember, "The Force is with you!"

Your gut sense is part of the split second firings of your entire neural system. Who says so? Research by Nobel Laureate professor of psychology and computer science Herbert Simon and his colleagues found that intuition reflects what you have learned and stored. Just because it comes in a flash, seemingly from nowhere, does not make it untrustworthy.

Simon said intuition emerges from the stored connections, or chunks, of experiences, facts, opinions, information, emotions, and other patterns of meaning culled from life experiences. When new information is integrated into an existing, related or new chunk, it can become available to consciousness to help you deal better with more complex situations.

More recent research about how information is processed complements Simon's work. "Predictive coding" identified in six-month-old babies suggests the brain has abstract models of the world that notes when something happens that doesn't fit. In other words, it responds to what doesn't happen as well as to what does, somewhat in a Sherlock Holmes mode. (For more on this, see Alison Gopnik's 2015 *Wall Street Journal* article, *The Curious Incident of the Baby in the Lab* at: http://on.wsj.com/1LblLUk.

These seemingly automatic, yet proven processes do not mean that you should avoid using your important reasoning powers. But they suggest strongly that ignoring your gut feeling can limit full access to the range of your internal resources, such as what's available beyond your brain. So take full advantage of your powers to avoid detours and wrong turns as well as to be more effective!

# FROM DISTRACTION TO FOCUS

How will you make sure you actually listen to, integrate, and act on what your gut tells you? One way is to respect and heed your first reaction, such as goose pimples from an exciting or dangerous experience. Nonverbal cues and general impressions provide additional information. In contrast, when you try too hard to figure things out, to rationalize everything, you can miss the essence or spirit of something. That may also distract you from what's important to understand and do.

If you find your mind going into overdrive or repetitive thinking, move to something refreshing. Here are some refocusing possibilities:

- Listen to some soothing music.
- Go for a walk or sit in a quiet, beautiful setting and meditate.
- Do some physical exercise you enjoy.

- Read something that intrigues you or captures your imagination.
- Have a conversation with an interesting person who's also a good listener .

As your mind calms, be alert to what emerges next. You can always return to your original thoughts. But they may seem somewhat stale from repetition in comparison to the fresher focus that becomes apparent from merging intuition and logic.

Another approach is to flirt with whatever your intuition suggests. Ask yourself out of the blue, what do you really, really want. Jot down the first words or phrases that pop into your head. For under five minutes, repeat that process once a day for three days running, more or less at the same time for consistency. Does what you've written tell you something inspiring and viable enough to trust as a basis for action?

# FROM INTUITION TO ACTION

Integrate what your intuition tells you with current related feelings, facts, and ideas. The results will likely give you some well-founded answers, or at least a direction for dealing with problems, issues, and blocks. With Albert Einstein, have faith in what you've learned in the process of living.

Einstein said "the only source of knowledge is experience." Even more apropos to this guide, he also said "The intuitive mind is a sacred gift and the rational mind a faithful servant. We have created a society that honors the servant and has forgotten the gift." For a more recent view directly related to the definition of courage I developed through my research, Steve Jobs said "Have the courage to follow your heart and intuition. They somehow already know what you truly want to become."

# FOR ADDITIONAL INSIGHT, LEARNING, AND GUIDANCE

**Choose a few sources that relate to your interests and situation.**

*Awakening Intuition* by Frances E. Vaughan

*Cracking the Intuition Code: Understanding and Mastering Your Intuitive Power* by Gail Ferguson

*Emotional Intelligence: Why It Can Matter More Than IQ by Daniel P. Goleman*

*Descartes' Error: Emotion, Reason and the Human Brain* by Antonio R. Damasio

*SQ: Connecting with Our Spiritual Intelligence* by Danah Zohar and Ian Marshall

*The Feeling of What Happens: Body and Emotion in the Making of Consciousness* by Antonio R. Damasio

*How Brains Make Up Their Minds* by Walter J. Freeman

*Gut Feelings: The Intelligence of the Unconscious* by Gerd Gigerenzer

*Blink: The Power of Thinking Without Thinking* by Malcolm Gladwell

http://video.pbs.org/video/2365600519/ - The Brain with David Eagleman

*The Brain Electric* by Malcolm Gay

*When Gut Bacteria Change Brain Function* by David Kohn
http://www.theatlantic.com/health/archive/2015/06/gut-bacteria-on-the-brain/395918/

Visual Intelligence: Sharpen Your Perception, Change Your Life by Amy E. Herman

*Different styles and people all can contribute to problem solving.*

## GUIDE TWO: WAYS TO UNTANGLE PROBLEMS

*"What we're saying today is that you're either part of the solution or you're part of the problem."*

~ Eldridge Cleaver, American writer, political activist, Black Panther leader; later a conservative Republican and possibly Mormon ~

# PREPARATION

20 minutes to read and choose a problem solving process to adapt and try out

# INGREDIENTS

Clarifying problem context and constraints

Adapting processes to fit needs

Having reasonable expectations and patience

Collaborating with appropriate people

# LIKELY RESULTS OF YOUR EFFORTS

Clarity about what's possible to accomplish

Avoidance of unproductive repetition and detours

Amelioration of problems

## OVERVIEW AND OPPORTUNITIES

Despite Cleaver's quote above, you can be part of the problem as well as the solution. Use this guide to address problems related to work, though the basic ideas can be adapted to personal life. In part that's because problem solving often involves generic processes that just require some tweaking for varying situations. Opportunities also lie in adjusting purely rational, linear versions to real life. By consciously integrating intuition and emotion into your approach, you'll have a better chance to improve outcomes.

Positive emotions help focus direction and organize actions. Intuition brings another level of insight that can augment as well as transcend logic. In fact, you probably know from experience that ignoring intuition may result in detours and wrong turns.

Current negative emotions or moods related to fear and anxiety may distort thinking and action. When you sense they lurk in the background, best to clarify their genesis and basis before letting them infiltrate your behavior and choices. Examples of such barriers to effectiveness can be reflected in:

- impulsiveness
- over-intellectualization
- physical symptoms related to stress
- inhibitions that seem out of proportion to capacities
- repetitive return to the same mental territory without progress or new insight

Whether you actually solve a problem, ameliorate, reframe, or eventually let it go, the more promising results are likely to occur when you deal with something that has meaning to you. That focus and inspiration will help you transcend blocks to moving forward. Joining with people who have similar values and concerns also improves the process and results. That's even better when they have different perspectives and skills that complement yours and support critical thinking and creativity.

In sum, more effective processes for problem solving are usually holistic, involving mind, heart, and gut feeling, or what some people call intuition. Your creativity and power flourish from playing with ideas, letting go of rigid expectations, and infusing appropriate discipline. As Franklin D. Roosevelt said, "There are many ways of going forward, but only one way of standing still."

# PROBLEMS ARE NOT ALWAYS SOLVABLE

Before plowing ahead, first ask yourself if the problem is worth addressing and whether you have appropriate means to work through it. Such means may include time, resources, influence, interest, skills, and commitment. Other matters to address are:

- Do you value and care enough about the matter to see it through?
- How complex is the interaction among its elements and the people involved?
- Is there a critical mass of stakeholders willing to invest in making progress that could benefit almost everyone?

Depending on your responses to the questions above, maybe the problem can just be made less bad. Perhaps the timing is not good for dealing with it. For example, people are not ready, or the situation is not yet ripe. Or maybe nothing can really be done.

Also beware of situations when only a minority is willing to grapple with the problem. As you've no doubt experienced, the process for solving something worth tackling usually requires the commitment of a critical mass of those involved. More basically daunting, though, are wicked problems that are so complex they can defy solution except possibly in the longer run. That could be when collaboration and commitment are led and managed effectively — and most of those affected see they have little choice but to commit to support their own interests and sustainability.

Examples of wicked problems are climate change and terrorism. Even if fully understood, the complexity of such problems means that addressing one aspect of it may lead to negative side effects and entanglements. For additional information, see https://en.wikipedia.org/wiki/Wicked_problem

To test whether or not a problem is manageable or even solvable, imagine the most viable strategies and what would happen as you tried the more promising ones or combinations. When the problem is complex, identify and explore at least briefly the results of other people's efforts in your or similar circumstances. Although you may subscribe to the idea that sustained effort conquers all, sometimes a more laissez faire approach can allow time, patience, and external influences to work their ways. While you're exploring options, consider how willing you are to deal with often messy ups and downs of situations you might choose to address.

Ultimately, stay open to a wider range of thinking, collaborations, and possible outcomes. Then you are more likely to anticipate what might get in the way and how you could make course corrections. This level of awareness and prior exploration also helps avoid disappointments and wastes of time.

## FIRST, DESCRIBE THE PROBLEM ACCURATELY

Although your view may shift and even change once you get involved with the problem solving process and begin to see possibilities, often the very definition of a problem dictates how you will proceed. That clarification can lead to better outcomes and suggest opportunities for amelioration or solution. For example, if I define a problem as "I don't get enough exercise," I would focus on types of exercises and timing, perhaps eliminating other apt activities. But if I say the problem is "How can I take better care of my body?" I would consider a range of healthy choices such as exercise, massage, bio-feedback, and good nutrition.

Another situation may involve a leader or manager, originally successful, but unable or unwilling to adapt to new challenges. You could define the problem from several perspectives: yours, the person's, or the organization's. If you have fewer options or less power, a possible attitude is to blame the person in charge for running the organization down. Then, three possible options for addressing the problem may be:

- Speak up in ways that don't sabotage yourself and yet make a contribution.

- Be quiet and hunker down, accepting the realities.

- Negotiate a better situation for yourself or leave if necessary.

But would any of them solve the problem of the ineffective person in charge? Maybe not, but they do provide choices that help you and possibly others progress or, at least, make peace with the situation. As you've learned from experience, changing another person is difficult if not impossible. You may be able to influence or help someone else, but the basic shift must come from within the individual who sometimes needs to hit bottom before addressing blocks, issues, or problems.

So probably the most promising strategy in problem solving is being and staying clear about exactly what the problem is, defining it in a way that encourages possible, viable outcomes for yourself and others who are affected. Here's Franklin Roosevelt again: "It isn't sufficient just to want — you've got to ask yourself what you are going to do to get the things you want."

To dig further into the realities implicit in a problem you face, take a few minutes now to explore any of the following questions::

- What opportunities lie in the problem for you and other people involved?

- Which specific aspects could actually be improved with at least small steps and which are intractable or beyond your influence?

- What are the win-win possibilities when conflict is present?

- How do conflict avoidance and other interpersonal and communication issues create barriers to progress?

- What do you need to let go (e.g. expectations, ego, pride, connections, attitudes issues, unbridled optimism, pessimism, one-right-way mentality)?

# UNCOVER PROBLEM COMPLEXITY AND LAYERS

Since problems often have multiple sources and dynamic aspects, start by considering the key descriptors that apply to your situation in Figure 1.1. below. Check at the left any related problem types to help you clarify your actual definition and situation. Add other descriptors in the spaces provided. Finally, circle or highlight the top four to seven descriptors that you think capture the main foundations or sources of the problem that will help you write a focused definition.

Figure 1.1 - Key Word List of Possible Problem Sources

| | |
|---|---|
| _____ Environmental | _____ Methodological |
| _____ Institutional | _____ Political |
| _____ Organizational | _____ Economic |
| _____ Group | _____ Social |
| _____ Personal | _____ Financial |
| _____ Situational | _____ Resource availability or use |
| _____ Future | _____ Psychological |
| _____ Present | _____ Interpersonal |
| _____ Past (inherited, historical) | _____ Managerial |
| _____ Transitory | _____ Leadership |
| _____ Permanent | _____ Familial |
| _____ Cultural | _____ Individual |
| _____ Values conflict | _____ Community or communal |
| _____ Goals conflict | _____ _____ |
| _____ Perceptual | _____ _____ |

40

_____ Gaps in information          _____ _____

To continue improving clarity, describe how the problem seems to you now. In no more than several sentences for focus, write your current definition of the problem below. This can be a challenge because many aspects can be interactive rather than founded on one static source. Yet try to be as clear and specific as possible as you capture what is likely natural complexity in the spaces provided here.

_____

_____

_____

_____

_____

Another useful way to refine your definition of the problem is to survey your scene on your own and with others. That can provide a sense of what to expect and preliminary data for problem solving. Consider using or adapting any of these methods and others that interest you.

- observation of the situation, noting themes, trends, anomalies, and paradoxes
- focus groups (diverse people brought together to improve clarity through guided discussion about a particular matter)
- quantitative and qualitative research and analysis
- interviews
- critical incidents you identify when doing story analysis
- surveys and questionnaires

Though ideas about the nature of the problem and ways to address it may emerge from collecting such data, avoid replacing action with continuing study. More is not always better. Whatever you decide to do, though, use relevant findings to improve the initial definition of the problem you wrote above.

## NO ONE BEST WAY: PROCESSES TO CONSIDER

Now that you've captured the nature of problem you want to address in several sentences, which aspects do you think can be influenced for the better and which are beyond reach? As you consider the range of processes to adapt and use below, let your tentative conclusions about what you can actually do help make choices for action. To focus on what's important, here's Franklin D. Roosevelt again: "Rules are not necessarily sacred, principles are."

To continue moving forward, perhaps join with some appealing people you respect to discuss and improve your understanding of the problem at various key points. Even definitions may become modified with such conversation and exploration. Certainly include representatives of stakeholders and other individuals who will be involved with implementation. From your own experience, you know commitment occurs when those affected by changes and actions have a hand in planning and decision making. In fact, that process of consultation and involvement can contribute to the problem solving implementation itself.

Throughout, allow adequate time for dealing with the complexity of the problem, resources, and natural rhythms of the people involved. Perhaps adding about 25% more time than you think necessary will give you wiggle room and avoid unnecessary pressure. Ask the people involved for their take on the time necessary as well.

You'll notice that the processes and methods below are presented in linear steps. Feel free to make common sense changes in any approach, adapting the sequencing to your situation, preference, and realities you encounter. If you wish, create diagrams and other images to capture the dynamics and inter-relationships. Identify, test, and use relevant, manageable software for efficiency and effectiveness. Finally, be alert for ways to integrate steps of more than one problem solving process suggested below.

# GROUP BRAINSTORMING: FOCUSING AND FOLLOW-UP

1. Define the problem with the people affected, encouraging open, shared discussion in person and online of the issues without judgment and evaluation.
2. Generate and capture suggestions for solving the problem, again facilitating open discussion and exploration.
3. Identify the consequences or advantages and disadvantages of each suggestion.
4. Choose and describe a course of action using analysis, synthesis, and intuition.
5. Anticipate and address, as possible, any strong emotions and self-interested responses that could distort or intrude on choices, priorities, and effective action steps.

6. Determine criteria for assessing agreed-upon outcomes, using qualitative and quantitative measures; capture before and after data.
7. Design the action plan with manageable steps, specified resources, evaluation methods, and approximate timing, among other considerations that make sense to you.
8. As you implement the action plan, use the information that emerges to refine understanding of the problem and anticipated consequences of a possible solution. Continue making worthwhile adjustments as you go.
9. Evaluate at appropriate points, as well as at the end, to continue making course corrections and for effective learning. Share the process and what you've uncovered with stakeholders and original contributors.

# CASE ANALYSIS APPROACH TO PROBLEM SOLVING

1. Identify the problem based on the written description of a situation in the case.
2. Determine all important, relevant facts and information that affect the problem.
3. Explore non-rational influences and considerations.
4. Specify main alternative solutions and their consequences.
5. Evaluate a few preferred alternative solutions for viability and fit with the situation, goals, and culture.
6. Recommend a solution or best alternative action with rationale for choice.

# CONVENTIONAL RESEARCH APPROACH

1. Identify the problem or purpose for study of the problem in collaboration with appropriate colleagues and other guiding professionals. (Continue communication throughout the process.)
2. Establish baselines of information from the start for later comparison with various results.
3. Specify dependent variables.
4. Specify independent variables.
5. Develop appropriate research methodology for the study, analyzing strengths, weaknesses, and tradeoffs.
6. Adjust methodological choice to make it more effective, appropriate, and manageable.

7.  Gather data using a variety of techniques to ensure you've captured the most relevant aspects, including outliers. Explore effective options for analysis and synthesis as well.

8.  Summarize results (or outcomes) and implications for future action related to the situation studied and perhaps similar ones.

9.  Present results and solicit feedback; answer questions, and use critiques for improving the analysis, synthesis, insights, and conclusions.

10. Choose follow up priorities and actions; move forward based on research results, potential user needs, and range of applications.

## APPROACH FOR RESOURCE-BASED PROBLEMS

1.  Problem Identification: State what the problem is, why it is a problem, and who and/or what causes or contributes to it.

2.  Goal Setting: Express simply what you want to accomplish, making sure each goal is related to the problem as you and those affected have defined it.

3.  Resource Identification: Identify the types of tangible and intangible resources that can help in reaching agreed upon goals. Explore all internal and external sources available that can actually provide support.

4.  Resource Allocation: Show how each resource will be used or earmarked for accomplishing each goal or sub-goal, if useful.

5.  Plan implementation: Outline steps needed to accomplish goals, identifying objectives and resources for each step. Specify anticipated issues, barriers, and opportunities. Imagine what you'll do to address possible intrusions and complications.

6.  Evaluation in Process: Define ways to monitor progress and do ongoing corrections or improvements.

7.  Actual implementation: Follow and adjust time line for putting action steps into effect.

8.  Evaluation: Assess outcomes and ways to improve the process; solicit ideas from stakeholders, participants, and contributors.

9.  Review and adjust process after discussing it informally or formally with sources of support, implementers, and clients. Keep moving forward with effective use of resources and identification of additional assistance as needed.

## GENERIC PROBLEM SOLVING

1.  Identify the problem.
2.  Set goal(s) for addressing the problem.
3.  Explore range of alternative, practical actions that will meet goals.

4. Evaluate alternative actions in relation to goal(s), resources (tangible and intangible), and barriers to implementation.
5. Choose best action(s) to reach each goal.
6. Describe consequences related to chosen actions and how they'd affect objectives in (7).
7. Determine objectives (concrete steps to meet each goal, based on preferred actions).
8. Implement.
9. Monitor and evaluate.
10. Use information from monitoring and evaluation to make modifications in approach during the process and in future applications.

# CONCLUSIONS

As you can see, the various processes for problem solving above are not mutually exclusive; there is a great deal of natural overlap. After considering them, develop your own version that integrates any of the ideas in a process that works for you and the people involved. Play with designing flow charts, diagrams, and other images. Use or adapt the most simple software that can capture the dynamism of planned processes and emerging realities.

Make sure that your choice reflects your true goals, time frame, and actual resources, whether they be less tangible such as cultural values or concrete such as money. Ask yourself throughout the process what the common sense, viable way forward is. Finally, to retain your sense of humor through what can be trying as well as stimulating experiences, consider poet and cartoonist Piet Hein's guidance:

"Problems worthy
of attack
prove their worth
by hitting back."

# FOR ADDITIONAL INSIGHT, LEARNING AND GUIDANCE

**Choose a few sources that relate to your interests and situation.**

*Mindmapping: Your Personal Guide to Exploring Creativity and Problem-Solving* by Joyce Wycoff

*Solving Tough Problems: An Open Way of Talking, Listening and Creating New Realities* by Adam Kahane

*Rapid Problem Solving with Post-It Notes* by David Straker

*Creative Problem Solving: An Introduction* by Donald J. Treffinger

*Creative Problem Solving: The Door to Individual Success and Change* by Thomas W. Dombroski

*Figuring Things Out: A Trainer's Guide to Needs and Task Analysis* by Ron Zemke and Thomas Kramlinger

*Descartes' Error: Emotion, Reason and the Human Brain* by Antonio R. Damasio

*Applied Minds: How Engineers Think* by Guru Madhavan

*Situational Analysis: Grounded Theory After the Postmodern Turn* by Adele E. Clarke

*Styles of Thinking: Strategies for Asking Questions, Making Decisions, and Solving Problems* by Allen F. Harrison and Robert M. Bramson

*Nonsense: The Power of Not Knowing* by James Holmes

*Doing Research to Learn about Effectiveness of Your Efforts and Client Development (Focus on Qualitative Research)* by Ruth M. Schimel at http://www.theschimellode.net/documents/DoingResearchaboutNonprofitEffectiveness.pdf

http://www.pbs.org/newshour/spc/character/essays/roosevelt.html

http://wagner.nyu.edu/courses/padm-gp.2145 - Design thinking as a creative approach to problem solving

*Strategy Development: A Process to Promote Your Vision* (in Ruth Schimel's blog) http://www.ruthschimel.com/strategy-development-a-process-to-promote-your-vision/

*Why Solve the Unsolvable?* by Sue Shellenberger, Wall Street Journal, February 24, 2016, p. D1: http://on.wsj.com/21okelM

*Smarter, Better, Faster* by Charles Duhigg

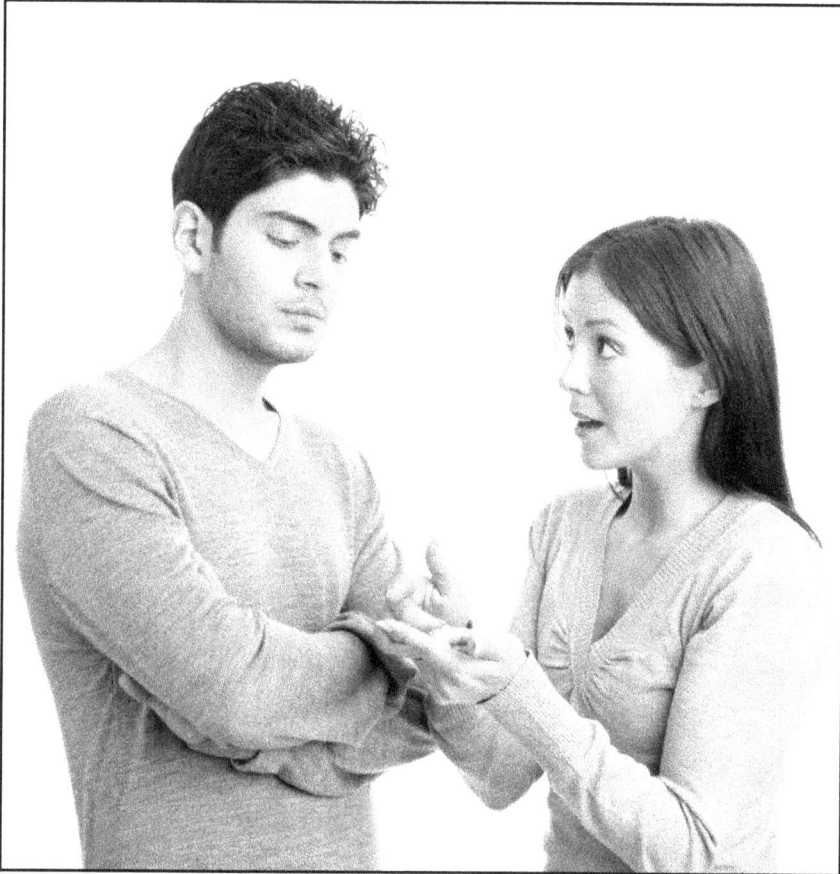

*Don't let negative nonverbal communication intimidate you.*

## GUIDE THREE: MANAGE RELATIONSHIP SABOTEURS

*"Personal relations are the important thing forever and ever, and not this outer life of telegrams and anger."*

~ E. M. Forster, 20th century English novelist and essayist ~

# PREPARATION

15 minutes to read and choose an application

# INGREDIENTS

Making interpersonal reactions and habits work in your favor

Marshaling your emotional and intellectual resources

Imagining opportunities for influence

# LIKELY RESULTS OF YOUR EFFORTS

Ability to transcend demeaning or limiting situations

Improved confidence

Stronger interpersonal skills

Better balance and sense of humor

## SITUATIONS THAT HARBOR SABOTEURS

In contrast to resources in Forster's 20th century Britain, modern tools of communication are rich with technological choices. They now include video conferencing, smart phones, social networking sites, texting, Skype, endless apps, and, of course, email. But what actually happens between people in face-to-face contact may not have changed that much. Some individuals still prompt anger, fear, anxiety, or even suffering. Experiences with them can drain your confidence, hope, and energy. Yet they also provide laboratories and opportunities to strengthen your own skills and courage.

This guide provides choices for dealing with a range of saboteurs who squelch satisfying human connection. These people tend to be inaccessible, complaining, difficult to read and please, or reproachful. Worse examples are controlling, manipulative, or mean individuals. They put up barriers to mutual understanding and civility, thwarting pleasure and progress, whether in work, social, or intimate situations. Their presence and influence on you may diminish your relationships within and beyond current groups.

Work saboteurs can include:

- bosses and other managers
- colleagues
- subordinates
- clients
- contractors

Intimate and social saboteurs can include:

- family members
- lovers
- friends
- neighbors
- acquaintances
- service providers
- congregation and other community members

These people can put negative stamps on quality of life and experiences far beyond their worth. They focus attention on their needs, quirks, and natures instead of matters of mutual interest and benefit. They may also be black holes into which possibilities and energy disappear.

How do these saboteurs get and retain their power? Whether in continuing or transitory situations, consciously or unconsciously, they know how to intimidate, distract, and use others. Unfortunately, their success in getting what they want using methods that have worked for them means they will likely continue their behaviors. But you still have choices about what you do and say.

When such exploitive, unpleasant, or disrespectful people are present in your life, adapt and use this guide to renew your peace of mind and create better outcomes for yourself and others. You may not always get the results you seek, but in time you'll make more progress than if you succumb to the saboteurs by allowing them to "hang out" in your mind and life or unbalance you. Whatever happens, you'll feel better taking the initiative, protecting yourself, and serving your needs.

# MENU FOR MANAGING SABOTEURS

### DESCRIBE THE SITUATION

When you sense you are in thrall to a draining or dangerous personal or professional relationship, start with specifying main details of what occurs instead of continuing to let it distract, sap strengths, or distort goals. Describe a typical situation briefly below, including what the person does, what you do, and your feelings about what tends to occur. (Focusing primarily on events, rather than what the saboteur evokes in you, can help free you from an often futile wish to change her or his behavior.)

_____

_____

_____

_____

_____

With this somewhat detached point of view, you can start to escape the saboteur's tentacles. Such people are often unhealthy, unhappy, or insecure; they prefer to keep others off balance. Some may even have significant mental health issues. In any event, they don't deserve your giving your time, attention, or power to them.

After briefly considering the description you wrote — which may provide some ventilation or release in itself — skim the suggestions below. Take the initiative by trying, adjusting, and integrating any of them. Make effective combinations that focus on the situation at hand and related ones. Bring your choices and own ideas together at the end. Whatever you decide, place your authentic stamp on what you do.

### MANAGE YOUR OWN LIMITING HABITS

Identify whatever behaviors you tend to have that could get in the way of a better outcome. Mention and adapt any of the following that apply and add your own ideas in the space at the end.

- thinking in repetitive, negative patterns
- avoiding asking for appropriate help, emotional as well as material
- imagining the worst results of your assertiveness
- acting impulsively or not at all

- avoiding useful conflict or self-assertion
- over-dramatizing
- reacting in the moment instead of making or insisting on some time to prepare yourself for effective communication and action

_____

_____

_____

How will you minimize the influence of your most unproductive tendency above that thwarts dealing with the saboteur and the goals you seek? Jot down some specific ideas below:

_____

_____

_____

Now that you've considered and committed to at least one way to re-focus your own behaviors in your favor, see what you think of the following ideas and actions for moving forward. Adapt them by all means you have at hand as well as what you can find and develop.

### STRATEGIES FOR CONTINUING PROGRESS

***Express your fears and anxieties to yourself first.*** Be explicit below about what troubles you in dealing this person. How do situations and experiences from your past relate to and affect this one? To empower yourself, re-visit similar occasions when you have come through well; consider how to adapt those actions to this situation now. Possibly check out your perspective with someone familiar with what's going on and interested in your welfare. Jot down below some ideas and at least one action you'll take within a week.

_____

_____

_____

***Gather hidden clues and cues.*** Sometimes the apparent negativity of the saboteur reflects vulnerability, lack of confidence, inadequate socialization, or difficult life history and current circumstances. While not accepting such information as an excuse, understanding the person may help you feel some compassion. It will also provide data for your own protection and hints about how to effectively breach the individual's facade — assuming that's worth your bother.

***Keep specifying what you can and want to accomplish.*** State below both the minimally acceptable and optimal outcomes you seek. By being clear about your goals for addressing the situation, you'll have a basis for organizing actions, resources, and expectations; you'll also be more likely to make better progress over time. That's assuming anything more than distancing or isolating yourself from the person or situation is appropriate.

_____

_____

_____

***Continue gathering information for effective management.*** Once you identify trustworthy sources, keep collecting and integrating information about the situation and person to use for communication and strategy. In addition to your stated goals, examples of data relate to underlying issues, other people's experiences with the person, and the concrete strengths you bring to the situation. Imagine how you will create situations to your advantage and follow through. Jot down any relevant ideas for action here.

_____

_____

_____

_____

***Pull your own support team together.*** Who can be in your corner? Identify who has relevant insight, authority, and influence and how you will ask them to help ameliorate the situation. Perhaps they can model effective behaviors, role play, brainstorm, explore strategies, or cheerlead. They may even provide some powerful backing.

Ask yourself, what's in it for each team member to assist you and what you will offer in return that will suit their needs and interests. Certainly a handwritten thank you note with specifics about the results of their help will show your gratitude. Even better, stay alert for ways to provide information and contacts that relate to your team members' situations. Finally, how else can you join with others outside the situation to serve your interests, get ideas, and possibly marshal additional support? Mention specific actions you will take here:

_____

_____

_____

***Practice what you want to say and how you'll say it.*** Gear your nonverbal behavior, such as eye contact, speed of communication and tone of voice, to support your goals for addressing the saboteur. Prepare several related open-ended questions starting with "what" and "how," and closed-ended questions that would elicit responses of a few words. Practice being comfortable with silence and other listening skills such as paraphrasing and reflection of feeling. (See the guide on listening skills in *Choose Courage In Your Relationships: Empower Yourself First*)

In addition, benefit from hearing yourself when you record a role play with someone who will do it with you realistically. Mention some key actions you'll take below, including how you could confidently excuse yourself from a situation with the saboteur or merely avoid it.

_____

_____

_____

***Choose additional effective communication strategies.*** Explore a range of possibilities to expand your options, deciding which ones work best for typical anticipated situations. Examples include face-to-face conversations in private, meetings and group discussions, emails, tapes, recordings, telephone chats, conference calls, texts, and letters. Imagine how you could use confident humor to brush off or diffuse situations. Identify your strategies, priorities, and choices below as well as related skills you want to strengthen.

***Take notes during exchanges or right afterward.*** This not only helps you remember actual statements, but is a good learning process that provides catharsis. It's also a record and reality test for developing personal insights and future strategy. Specify how you'll capture that data in detail below along with main issues and themes you expect to encounter.

_____

_____

_____

***Prepare to handle a range of outcomes.*** Whether you expect negative, neutral, or positive experiences, identify briefly ways to maintain your dignity and keep the line of communication open, as you wish.  What is the worst scenario you can imagine? How would you deal with it, behaviorally, intellectually, and emotionally? Do the same for neutral and positive scenarios.  Indicate briefly below your strategies.

_____

_____

_____

***Prepare for actual exchange with the saboteur.*** Whenever you face something challenging and possibly new, get into the mood — as good a one as possible. What activities would be healthy, pleasurable, or soothing?  Mention  some below and how you'll time them for best preparation before an exchange. Finally, what mantras could help? Examples are "what's the worst thing that can happen?" and "I will handle this because I know what I will do now and what I will  avoid."

_____

_____

_____

***Re-energize your sense of humor.***  Avoid taking the person, situation, and yourself too seriously. Is this a matter of life and death?   What's potentially amusing, silly — or even wasteful about over thinking it all? If the person is intimidating, imagine her or him in a compromising or very human situation such as taking a shower — or something more inelegant.  Describe briefly below examples of such images of the person or associations that come to mind which will make you laugh or smile.

_____

_____

_____

## STAYING READY FOR YOUR TOUCHDOWNS

Not all the choices you've made will unfold in neat, linear ways. With experience, let go of suggestions and ideas that don't work or are irrelevant. As you continue, you'll probably recognize that even considering and adjusting your choices will improve your confidence and prepare you for effective action. Continue with options that continue to be promising and make sense to you, possibly integrating some. One aim could be to make situations "less worse" in the short run.

To encourage your momentum, create your time line for action in the space below. Include start time, major intermediate steps, and finish time that's viable

_____

_____

_____

Who is really in the catbird seat now? You, of course, because you have a clearer perspective and definite goals as well as a variety of ways to get what you want. You're the person with the motivation and skills to act differently instead of reacting. You may even be doing Mr. or Ms. Saboteur a favor when they realize new possibilities for themselves in response to your actions. If not, it's their loss and your opportunity to see things realistically, choosing what you want to do next and how you want to handle yourself.

Since saboteurs can fade or go away and new ones appear, keep using these suggestions and your own ideas to add to your confidence. Remind yourself of each situation you handle that makes you proud and what you have learned in order to face the next challenge. Acknowledge any progress, including how you've avoided repeating unproductive situations and behavioral tendencies.

For reinforcement and encouragement, read articles and books that inform and guide you in dealing with relationship saboteurs. Also explore fictional sources such as novels, short stories, plays, and soap operas with related casts of characters and situations. They can be just as educational and often more stimulating, inspiring, and fun as you experiment with authentic ways to express your influence and powers. Finally, explore online guidance and resources using key words such as:

- narcissists
- insecure people

- difficult people
- mean people
- relationship saboteurs
- bullies
- manipulators

The sources below may also help, but don't substitute repetitive thinking, studying, and discussion for effective action.

# FOR ADDITIONAL INSIGHT, LEARNING AND GUIDANCE

## Choose a few sources that relate to your interests and situation.

*Making Peace with Yourself: Turning Your Weaknesses into Strengths* by Harold H. Bloomfield

*Dealing with People You Can't Stand: How to Bring Out the Best in People at Their Worst* by Rick Brinkman and Rick Kirschner

*Since Strangling Isn't an Option...: Dealing with Difficult People - Common Problems and Uncommon Solutions* by Sandra A. Crowe

*Thank You for Being Such a Pain: Spiritual Guidance for Dealing with Difficult People* by Mark I. Rosen

*Coping with Difficult People* by Robert M. Bramson

*How to Deal with Difficult People* by Paul G. Friedman

*When Difficult Relatives Happen to Good People* by Leonard Felder

*Choosing Civility: The 25 Rules of Considerate Conduct* by P.M. Forni

*Don't Worry: Why Repetitive Negative Thinking Is Bad for You* in August 11, 2015 *Wall Street Journal* by Shirley S. Wang: http://on.wsj.com/1NtMlsb

*Decide what's worth your effort to do.*

## GUIDE FOUR: TRANSCEND LIMITING SITUATIONS

*"Do what you can, with what you have, where you are."*

~ Theodore Roosevelt, U.S. President ~

## PREPARATION

20 minutes to read, describe your situation, and choose your next step

## INGREDIENTS

Staying open and optimistic

Considering alternatives

Persisting in working for what you want

Converting frustration, discomfort, or suffering into action

## LIKELY RESULTS OF YOUR EFFORTS

Fewer limitations and constraints

Increased energy and confidence

Time to devote to positive pursuits

Improved balance and perspective

Appreciation of strengths

## SEEDS FOR PROGRESS IN CHALLENGES

If it were easy to improve or leave difficult, unproductive, or unhealthy situations, you probably wouldn't be reading this. In fact, you may already be aware of the many contributing factors within you, others, and the environment that make such limiting situations hard to transcend. Yet your first step for improving your life can be relatively simple. Just use this guide to describe what is getting in your way and choose one related step to take now.

To start, look over the eight themes below. Then check any you relate to in the space to the left of the description, completing each one briefly in your own words. As appropriate, make adaptations in the descriptions to reflect your situation more closely. If you'd prefer to write your version from scratch, use the ninth option at the end. Among those you've chosen, put the top three in priority order, placing (1) next to the situation that's most significant to you. Your choices and descriptions will hold the seeds for improving your life.

____I don't get along with _____(boss, colleague, client, subordinate, neighbor, relative or ?) because:

_____

_____

_____

_____My companion has a pessimistic or limited approach to life, tending to complain or over-focus in particular about _____. My role has been:

_____

_____

_____

_____I dislike my work (or main activities) because:

_____

_____

_____

_____I do not feel capable of handling _____ because:

_____

_____

_____

_____I keep repeating _____
and seem unable to move forward because:

_____

_____

_____

_____I don't like my current situation, but can't express clearly what I want. This is how I've been dealing with this impasse so far:

_____

_____

_____

_____I'm in a relationship that's _____(unsatisfying, going nowhere, flat, one-way, rocky, problematic, abusive, unproductive, not in my interest, boring, or ?). So far, I've tried to deal with it by_____ _____, but have not yet made progress because:

_____

_____

_____

_____

_____ Family, work, community, or ? _____conflicts frustrate me.  I want the situation to change but _____

_____

_____

_____

_____ If none of the foregoing describe your situation, briefly describe your own major issue and what you've been able to do about it here:

_____

_____

_____

Below, on a separate paper, or whatever works for you, specify the most significant issue from your choices above in greater detail using your own words. To get yourself started, try using free association; jot down whatever key words and phrases pop into your head. For example, do they relate to attitudes, emotions, habits, reactions, styles, communication patterns, or pressures?

_____

_____

_____

_____

_____

After carefully considering your first chosen description, answer the following questions:

- What do you contribute to the situation?

_____

_____

_____

- Name one or two other  people who contribute to the situation and what each one does:

_____

_____

_____

- What significant environmental or situational influences, generally beyond your control, contribute to the situation?

_____

_____

_____

Notice that the word contribute, not cause, is used in the questions above. That's because in complex situations there is rarely one reason, source, or cause. Often factors are not only multiple, but also interactive.

Despite this complexity, you can still create better outcomes through the choices you make, especially when you start with yourself where you have most discretion for action. So after reviewing your chosen description of the situation and answers to the three questions in the bullets above, respond to any of the following that you think will be useful.

- What will you do to modify or change in your own behavior?

_____

_____

- What will you accept about yourself and/or others because you cannot or will not change it?

_____

_____

- What will you discuss or explore with _____ ?

_____

_____

To continue making progress:

- Specify below the most beneficial, manageable action you will take within the next week to influence the situation and serve your own interest. Schedule it with adequate time for the step(s) you plan.

_____

_____

- What concrete, accessible assistance, if any, makes sense to get?

_____

_____

- Looking ahead to the foreseeable future, name a longer-term goal and specify what, how, and when you plan to meet it. With each subsequent mini-move toward that goal, celebrate your progress. Along the way, avoid repetitive and self-defeating thoughts as much as possible, limiting them to no more than five to ten minutes daily.

_____

_____

_____

_____

After you have done everything you think you can and the situation has not improved, at least detach yourself from it in your mind for now. Sometimes just the passage of time can contribute to a better outcome. But if you think there is no hope, plan how you can best leave it altogether.

One way is to keep yourself from dwelling on the matter by substituting activities and relationships that are healthy. For example, experiment with the suggestions at the end. Possibly, even physically move away. If you find it difficult to do any of this or whatever else you think of yourself, complete any of the following below that will assist your progress:

- What is blocking you from letting go?

_____

_____

- How does holding on to this main block benefit you?

_____

_____

- How does holding on to this main block hurt you?

_____

_____

If you continue feeling blocked, talk it over with trusted people and/or write about it briefly in focused ways to avoid wallowing in repetitive thinking. Based on the insights that emerge, name below and follow through on one practical, accessible action you can take now. Continue acknowledging any progress you make. Sometimes progress is not linear or logical, but small steps can increase confidence and stimulate some modest results.

_____

_____

In those situations where you accept that you have inadequate or no influence, seek some collaborators among friends, family, colleagues, and professionals. Identify what can actually be accomplished under the circumstances and what they can do to assist you and vice versa. In conversation, identify specific ways you can leave the situation gracefully and safely, whether physically, emotionally, or in your thoughts. If the latter persist, keep replacing them with manageable productive ideas or pleasant distractions and move on.

If you find you're still stuck and avoiding action, don't be surprised. The complexity of the situation, the length of time you have been in it, and your own habits may not lead to rapid or clear progress. Rather than give up in frustration and stay stuck, though, just choose one small action you can take today. Try another one tomorrow. Whatever happens, don't stop moving ahead in appropriate ways. Each action will strengthen your rhythm of taking responsibility, adding to your self-respect, hope, and peace of mind.

Recognize, also, that finding possible and pleasant ways to vent your emotions, feelings, and frustrations can also help generate energy to move forward. Here are suggestions to use. Adapt and add to them as you wish.

- Do regular physical activitiess that are enjoyable and challenging, from dancing to sports.
- Sing at the top of your lungs or find other ways to release tension and express yourself.
- Substitute repetitive thinking with other ways to let out your feelings using words, color, design, line, or whatever else appeals.
- Pamper yourself regularly with simple choices such as restful, adequate sleep, deep breathing, meditation, and visualizing pleasures that don't require resources. Wallow in beauty as you define it, whether in nature, museums, or other sources that appeal.
- Remind yourself of how you successfully managed or left limiting situations before. Discover some role models for inspiration in person, on the page, online, or through the arts and humanities.
- Admit your vulnerabilities and challenges to only a few trustworthy people who can commiserate and understand your situation without giving unrequested advice or telling their stories — often monologs they think will help you. Sometimes what you say serves as a catharsis.
- Assume temporarily another identity that makes you smile such as imitating King Kong pounding his chest, other animal behavior, or a comic book character that brings out your imagination and possible powers such as Batman or Wonder Woman. (My own favorite is imitating the penguin's comic gait which makes me smile and feel playful.)

Finally, if you continue being stuck for too long a time, find it impossible to budge, or sense danger, you may not be able to find a way out on your own. Be especially alert to when you repeat unproductive or self-destructive patterns. That behavior will signal that you truly need to break out in healthier ways, probably with assistance from neutral observers and professionals trained to deal with situations like yours.

# FOR ADDITIONAL INSIGHT, LEARNING AND GUIDANCE

## Choose a few sources that relate to your interests and situation.

*The Protean Self: Human Resilience in an Age of Fragmentation* by Robert Jay Lifton

*Learned Optimism: How to Change Your Mind and Your Life* by Martin Seligman

*The Resilient Spirit: Transferring Suffering into Insight and Renewal* by Polly Young-Eisendrath

*The Survivor Personality: Why Some People Are Stronger, Smarter, and More Skillful at Handling Life's Difficulties ... and How You Can Be, Too* by Al Siebert and Bernie Siegel

*Resilience: The Power to Bounce Back When the Going Gets Tough* by Frederic Flach

*The Art of Resilience: 100 Paths to Wisdom and Strength in an Uncertain World* by Carol Orsborn

*The Resilient Self: How Survivors of Troubled Families Rise Above Adversity* by Steven J. Wolin

*The Dance of Intimacy: A Woman's Guide to Courageous Acts of Change in Key Relationships* by Harriet Lerner

*The Dance of Connection: How to Talk to Someone When You're Mad, Hurt, Frustrated, Insulted, Betrayed or Desperate* by Harriet Lerner

*Should You Leave?* by Peter D. Kramer

*Battered Women's Protective Strategies: Stronger Than You Know (Interpersonal Violence)* by Sherry Hamby

See Ruth's blogs at http://www.ruthschimel.com/blog/; http://www.ruthschimel.com/fantasy-and-fun-from-comics-for-your-progress/

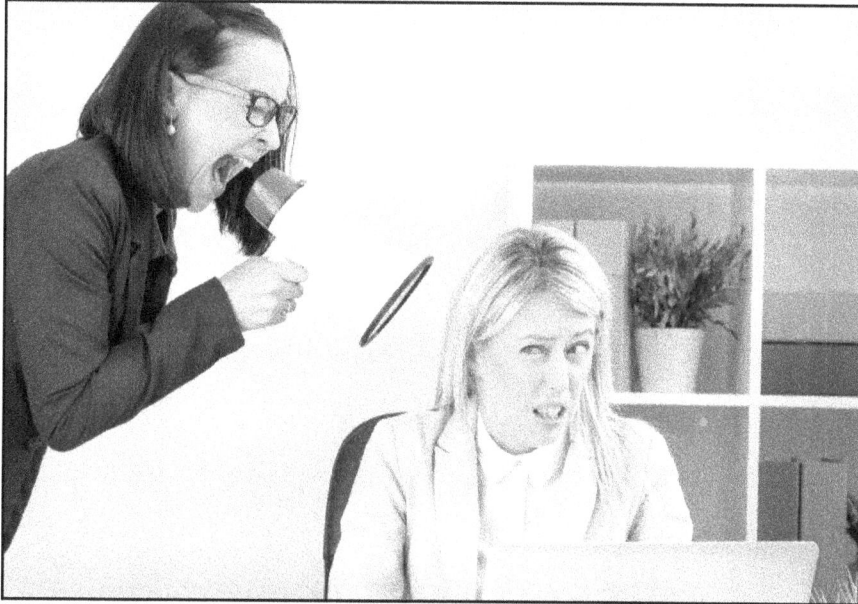

**You don't have to sit and take it.**

*"The place that seems most dangerous is exactly where safety lies."*

~ Barbara Cook, American singer and actress ~

## GUIDE FIVE: BLOCK THE BULLIES — WORK AND BEYOND

## PREPARATION

10 minutes to read, assess your situation, and use an aspect of *your* power

# INGREDIENTS

Admitting feeling threatened

Using your possibly unappreciated powers

Being willing to stand up for yourself

Meeting dangers directly

# LIKELY RESULTS OF YOUR EFFORTS

Effective self-protection

Safer situations

Greater self-respect

Renewed energy and hope

# THE BULLIES' SETUP

Bullies and other people who disrespect and hurt you can exist in families, schools, workplaces, online, in public places, and other contexts. If you are used to accommodating them, they already have some sway over you. Read further to find out how to loosen their grip.

In work and other situations, bullies are more likely to express their destructive behaviors through emotional harassment rather than physical abuse. But any abuse can hurt and weaken recipients' resolve. Below are examples of bosses and co-workers who engage in emotional harassment in varying degrees. They include people who can "hit" you with the following behaviors, one-on-one or even in groups. They:

- yell and scream
- accuse you of things that are not true
- keep you on the defensive
- find fault continually, never acknowledging your accomplishments
- ignore or disparage appropriate requests

They may also weaken your relationships with others and decrease your effectiveness in other ways. For example, they may:

- withhold necessary information or assistance, often providing it late if at all
- insist or force you do things that go against your values or interests
- require you to hurt or diminish others
- keep you in limbo about situations that affect you
- degrade you and others by using unprofessional or inappropriate language

Other destructive behaviors include:

- bad mouthing you to others
- carrying and telling tales that are upsetting or demeaning
- using sexual innuendo or making advances
- over controlling, including inflexible adherence to rules that could be adjusted
- lying about a variety of matters
- stealing credit for your accomplishments
- isolating you from other people and opportunities

# FALLOUT FROM BULLYING

Often, the longer you are exposed to such circumstances, the less confident you feel. Then, the likelihood of your negotiating, confronting, or leaving the situation is lessened. If you feel scared or think you have no alternative that could be a sign that the perpetrator has already inhibited your capacity for assertion and self-protection.

Briefly describe here your current state of mind as it relates to a "put-down person":

_____

_____

_____

Paradoxically, the place that seems most dangerous — the unknown future — is exactly where safety could lie for you. So stay open, or at least neutral, as you imagine what a shift away from present dangers and limiting situations could hold for you. Certainly the known present and how it would play out is predictable and demeaning enough to encourage you to take action, however modest, that could bring a change for the better.

# OPTIONS FOR DEALING WITH BULLIES NOW

However you describe your state of mind, start laying the groundwork for exiting gracefully and strongly. Even if leaving immediately is not possible, acting as if you could will strengthen your muscles for forward movement. Consider the following suggestions for self-protection and strengthening your position now. Adapt and add to them as you wish.

# DOCUMENT THE SITUATION

Keep brief, specific notes on everything that's relevant, such as descriptions of each occurrence: include behaviors toward you, dates, what you did and said, and how the other person responded. If there were observers, note their names and find out if they'd confirm to others what they saw and heard. In addition, identify patterns or catalysts of the bully's behavior. Mention whatever comes to mind below.

_____

_____

_____

_____

_____

# CONNECT WITH TRUSTWORTHY, SUPPORTIVE PEOPLE

Find out about partnerships and coalitions of people who have experiences similar to yours. Ask if they are willing to provide guidance or assist you. Among them or others, you may encounter mentors with whom to discuss the situation and choices for action. Stay alert to how you can thank and help them as well. Jot down your initial ideas here:

_____

_____

_____

As appropriate, identify people who would be willing to discuss the matter or at least brainstorm with you. Be prepared with some written notes about the situation to guide yourself. Have specific strategies ready to discuss since the person may want your ideas or prefer you to take the initiative. Ideally, anyone you talk to should have some formal or informal influence over the bully.

_____

_____

_____

In any conversation with people who have relevant authority, focus first on your own specific efforts to deal with the situation and what happened. Specify what you think is intentional infliction of emotional distress or damage. Avoid sounding whiny or showing you feel like a victim. Explore also what they are willing to do to influence, control, or even remove the person.

When appropriate, bring up how you might be removed from the situation in ways that are beneficial for you. During or afterwards, keep clear notes on what is said; they will be useful as catharsis, memory bank, and source of data should you seek assistance from third-parties such as an employment lawyer, mediator, union representative, or psychologist.

Specify your next action steps below after you've thought about these suggestions and what happened in any conversations. Be specific about what you want to do, who you'll contact, and when.

_____

_____

_____

# DEVELOP VIABLE, INDEPENDENT OPTIONS

Maybe it's time to concurrently explore or create opportunities for yourself within the current context and elsewhere that would remove you from exposure to the person as well as improve your situation. Outline an exit plan based on a preliminary, viable vision for your future. This could include describing a situation you'd prefer, exploring new opportunities, developing additional abilities and skills, and being ready with diplomatic, concrete reasons for leaving. Whatever happens and becomes possible, this exploration in itself can inspire and embolden you.

At the same time, engage in activities that will strengthen your confidence and prospects. For example, look into:

- participating in professional, religious, spiritual, and social groups that express your values and include people you're likely to appreciate and vice versa
- renewing friendships and connections with people you respect and enjoy
- joining social activities where you'll meet new individuals who could bring out the best in you and possibly stimulate or model fresh ways of thinking and acting
- learning and practicing new skills (e.g. negotiation and interpersonal) that strengthen your capacities to deal with your current situation and prepare you for the future
- doing anything you enjoy already and experimenting with related activities, professional as well as personal

Considering these ideas and your own, name one interesting activity you'd start and for which you'll block time on your calendar now. Mention below when, how, and with whom you will do this.

_____

_____

_____

## CONTINUING DANGERS AND OPPORTUNITIES

Whatever evolves and results from the foregoing approaches you've chosen to try, over thinking and discussing matters you don't control or can't even influence may very well gobble energy and time from taking action in your favor. As you've no doubt already experienced, wallowing in negative feelings just wears you down further. So while some conversation and strategy planning are important, stay alert to when they replace incremental action and impede progress.

To promote action, use a weekly calendar that allows you to block time for steps that are likely to meet your manageable goals. Use it to guide everyday action and check your progress. At the end of each week acknowledge what you've accomplished and learned as well as what needs adjusting. This can include anything from practical, seemingly ordinary matters to your vision for your future.

Be especially alert if your current circumstance reminds you of previous ones in which you've taken guff and worse. That previous conditioning can be a straight-jacket that keeps you static. Note below anything that comes to mind.

_____

_____

_____

At the same time, be alert to when bullies, being bullies and often cowards, back off if confronted. For example, you'll see in the link to bullyonline at the end of this guide that they tend to have consistent characteristics. Occasionally, when they become aware of the negative impact of their behavior or how it could affect their own status, they may even modify their behavior or retreat.

Nevertheless, you may understandably sense there is little hope for change or too much danger in confrontation. Perhaps you'll assume it's wasted effort to deal directly with the bully. Then, give yourself a practical time frame for finding a better situation or exiting altogether. Be clear in your own mind about what you will do in the interim. Describe several specific strategies below, including cultivating safe havens, literally or symbolically, support networks, and collaborators for support.

_____

_____

_____

During any static periods of which there could be many, imagine you're a duck letting the toxic spray from the person flow off your back. Sometimes an adequate response can be as simple as a direct stare as you move away, disapproving frown, wry smile, or some other subtle, yet strong, nonverbal response. Whatever you do, let it reflect your self-confidence and send a message that you're not intimidated. Or try paraphrasing whatever the person is saying, followed by your silence and sustaining a straightforward gaze. Perhaps experiment with that approach when you feel ready to see what happens. To bolster yourself, try giving the person the finger in your imagination.

While controlling the bully is unlikely, you can assert yourself and draw emotional and actual boundaries that work for you under the circumstances. Again, as you feel ready, specify what's not acceptable to you and what you'll do about it. Just make sure you can follow through on what you've thought or said. Continue to keep specific notes on what transpired.

Of course, if you're dealing with a cyber bullying situation, tactics and strategies need to be adapted. According to Pew Research, about 40% of online users have experienced bullying, harassment, and intimidation. (See link in sources at the end.) Although younger people have more experiences, women and minorities are thought to have it worse.

For additional guidance on dealing with this, Google cyber bullying to find a range of descriptions and advice. Choose and consider links that relate to your situation. In addition, investigate the latest court cases on cyber bullying which reflect the struggle between freedom of speech and freedom from harassment at state levels.

Finally, depending on your situation, consider using it as a laboratory for practicing more assertive behavior in general, whether in person or online. Whatever you decide, make sure it matches your stronger nature and values as well as what you are facing. Use or adapt these questions to make your next steps specific and productive:

- What is in my interest to do now?

_____

_____

- Who will help me proceed?

_____

_____

- How and when will I take productive action?

_____

_____

# FOR ADDITIONAL INSIGHT, LEARNING, AND GUIDANCE

## Choose a few sources that relate to your interests and situation.

*Who's Afraid of the Big, Bad Boss: 13 Types and How to Survive Them* by Marilyn Haight

*How to Work for an Idiot: Survive and Thrive --- Without Killing Your Boss* by John Hoover

*Take the Bully by the Horns: Stop Unethical, Uncooperative, or Unpleasant People from Running and Ruining Your Life* by Sam Horn

*The Bully at Work: What You Can Do to Stop the Hurt and Reclaim Your Dignity on the Job* by Gary Namie and Ruth Namie

*You Don't Have to Take It!: A Woman's Guide to Confronting Emotional Abuse at Work* by Ginny Nicarthy et al

*Bullies, Tyrants and Impossible People: How to Beat Them Without Joining Them* by Ronald M. Shapiro and Mark A. Jankowski

Workplace Bullying Institute: www.workplacebullying.org

http://www.adweek.com/socialtimes/new-study-finds-40-adults-cyberbullying/206682

http://bullyonline.org/workbully/serial_introduction.htm for characteristics of serial bullies.

*From an anonymous app, a forum for abuse* by Moriah Balingit in *The Washington Post*, December 9, 2015: http://wpo.st/5L-w0 - Relates to the After School app used by high school students

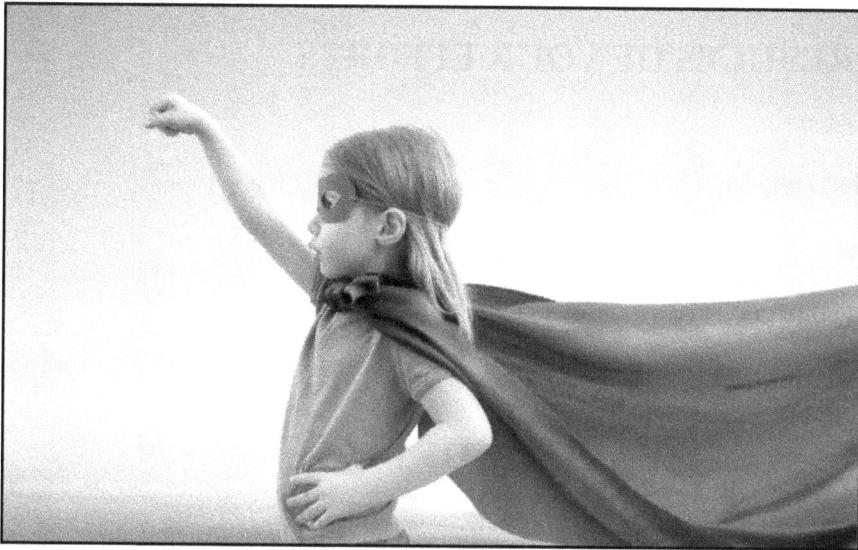

*Power comes in many forms. How will expand your choices?*

## GUIDE SIX: USE YOUR POWER — FULLY

*"The love of liberty is the love of others; the love of power is the love of ourselves."*

~ William Hazlitt, English writer, humanistic art and literary critic ~

## PREPARATION

15 minutes to read, give preliminary responses, and choose one action to take

## INGREDIENTS

Expanding your range of powers

Clarifying what power means to you

Imagining how you want to express your power

## LIKELY RESULTS OF YOUR EFFORTS

Saved time

Increased effectiveness

Clarity in relationships

Ease in using your power

Empowerment of others

# MEANINGS OF POWER

Power is an evocative word. Maybe you have positive, negative, or mixed associations with it. Whatever your associations, your attitude toward power can be a self-fulfilling prophecy. If you avoid using your own power or resist it in others, you could be in a passive or reactive mode. Opportunities for growth, use of talents, and satisfaction in work and other situations could be missed. So would the positive influence of power in many relationships. Use this guide to encourage productive use of the range of your powers.

The following information and questions are offered to help you explore your personal definitions of power. Once they are clear and comfortable for you, you will be more likely to use aspects of power that suit you well. You'll enjoy the fruits of your actions as well.

Management theorists have defined power according to its source. Examples are power founded on:

- **formal authority** or what comes with a particular position
- **coercion** or the capacity to punish, whether used or not
- **expertise** or the ability to do something well
- **rewards** and other ways to acknowledge the accomplishments of others
- **inspiration** of respect and emulation, an aspect of leadership

Among these five examples, list all key words that connect with your values:

_____
_____
_____

Which types of power do you tend to use and when?

_____
_____
_____

Which ones do you want to cultivate or at least explore?

_____
_____
_____

Which ones do you avoid using and why?

_____
_____
_____

To complete this exploration of your uses of power, answer in the spaces provided any of the following that you think will help you clarify your attitudes and promote effective actions.

- What significant experiences have you had with the misuse of power by yourself and others?

_____
_____
_____

- How do you tend to gain power?

_____
_____
_____

- How do you tend to lose power?

_____
_____
_____

- How and by whom is power taken from you?

_____
_____
_____

- How can you empower others?

_____
_____
_____

**Given your responses to the previous questions:**

- Identify below one manageable, worthwhile opportunity for developing or using an aspect of your power.

_____
_____
_____

- Mention briefly below a few specific steps you'll take and when you'll use the opportunity chosen in the previous bullet:

_____
_____
_____

- Who can help you? What will you say to them? When will you ask them? How will you acknowledge their assistance? Jot down your specific plan of action here:

_____

_____

_____

- What satisfying reward will you give yourself for the first time you use your power in a new, effective way?

_____

_____

_____

If you make any mistakes, use them as opportunities for learning. Indicate below what you would do to avoid dwelling too long on a mistake and what you would do to move on.

_____

_____

_____

Ultimately, an effective way to liberate yourself as well as others to use power well is to encourage the most ethical, responsible applications possible. Following the advice in the Hazlitt quote at the start of this guide, once you love yourself enough to express your own power in ways that suit you, your comfort with the process will increase. Helping others to use their power appropriately can strengthen your own process as well. Together, such mutual understanding will reinforce and improve shared activities, work, and goals.

## To start empowering others:

- Name one person in the space provided below whom you'd like to help expand or deepen their use of power. How will you describe to them your purpose for doing so?

_____

_____

_____

- How will you engage the person in the process? (For example, inform them of your motivation, guide them in exploring what power is and what it may mean to them, and create a plan together to meet an agreed upon objective or goal.) Indicate here the specific steps you'll take:

_____

_____

_____

- How will you know you've created satisfying outcomes that suit both of you?

_____

_____

_____

- How can you encourage the person to pass the process forward to others?

_____

_____

_____

The expansion and expression of your power depends in part on your willingness to develop and use your true capacities. In the process, you will make better progress in directions you want. You will also increase your confidence. Your own self-empowerment experiences will contribute to appreciating the ethical, effective exercise of power by others. That's one way you'll know that you've come to good terms with being powerful — in your unique way. Now, it's time to power up!

# FOR ADDITIONAL LEARNING, GUIDANCE, AND INSIGHT

## Choose a few sources that relate to your interests and situation.

*Kinds of Power: A Guide to Its Intelligent Uses* by James Hillman

*Power Talk: Using Language to Build Authority and Influence* by Sarah Myers McGinty

*Power and Influence: Beyond Formal Authority* by John P. Kotter

*The 3 Keys to Empowerment: Release the Power Within People for Astonishing Results* by Ken Blanchard et al

*The Facilitator's Fieldbook: Step-by-Step Procedures, Checklists and Guidelines, Samples and Templates* by Thomas Justice and David W. Jamieson

*How the Way We Talk Can Change the Way We Work: Seven Languages of Transformation* by Robert Kegan and Lisa Laskow Lahey

*The 48 Laws of Power* by Robert Greene

*Lessons for Shutting Down a Gronwup Cyber Bully* by Elizabeth Bernstein, *The Wall Street Journal* http://on.wsj.com/1staPoj

*The Prince* by Niccolo Machiavelli

*A Hobbit, A Wardrobe, and A Great War* by Joseph Locante

*The Three-Year Swim Club: The Untold Story of Maui's Sugar Ditch Kids and Their Quest for Olympic Glory* by Julie Checkoway

See Ruth's blog about Wonder Woman, among other powerful comic book icons: http://www.ruthschimel.com/fantasy-and-fun-from-comics-for-your-progress/

# INDEX

## A

acting as if.................................................. 74
action......................................................... 92
aggression in children............................... 7
agreement ......................................11, 14, 15
al Qaeda .................................................... 22
ambivalence about conflict ..................... 12
American cultural values .................... 23, 24
analysis .........................16, 24, 42, 43, 44
anxiety .......................... 1, 22, 26, 27, 37, 50, 92, 95
assertive behavior .................................... 78
assessment format ..................................... 3
assumptions .........................9, 17, 24, 27
authenticity ................................................ 92

## B

barriers to effectiveness........................... 38
baselines.................................................... 44
behavioral filters........................................ 7
being stuck ................................................ 67
boundaries.................................................iv
Brown, Emma ............................................. 2
browning of America ................................. 23
bullies .......................................28, 72, 79

## C

case............................................................ 44
cause and effect ........................................ 24
change ..........................8, 23, 39, 52, 63, 64, 73, 77
clues .......................................................... 53
coercion..................................................... 81
collaboration ............................6, 13, 15, 22, 39, 44
complex situations ......................18, 32, 64

complexity ............................ 7, 24, 39, 42-43, 64, 66
conflict ......................... 4, 5, 8-14, 17, 20-22, 40, 52
conflict resolution ............................... 10, 13
consequences ......................................43-45
consistency ........................................... 8, 33
courage .................................................93-98
cultural differences......................20-23, 25
culture........................................................ 20
current capabilities .................................... 1
cyber bullying............................................77-78

## D

definitions of power ................................. 81
Deresiewicz, William................................ 21
destructive behaviors .........................72-73
discomfort ................................................. 92
disrespect .................................................. 72
distraction.................................................. 32
domestic issues......................................... 23
domestic violence and terrorism.......... 22

## E

emotional harassment.............................. 72
emotions.................................................... 93
Einstein, Albert ........................................ 34
empowering others .............................83-84
enjoy cultural variety ............................... 25
epigenetics................................................. 7
evaluate ............................................... 44, 45
exit, voice, and loyalty ............................... 8
expectations .........................8, 11, 26, 37, 38, 41, 54
experiences...8, 12, 20, 32, 46, 53-56, 74, 78, 82, 85
expertise ..................................... 3, 18, 81

## F

fear...........................1, 22, 23, 25, 27, 37, 50, 92, 95
first reaction.........................................................32
formal authority..................................................81
futile wish ...........................................................52

## G

gain power ...........................................................82
generate energy...................................................67
Generic Problem Solving.......................................45
genes.....................................................................7
getting to yes ................................................15, 17
good outcomes ...............................................1, 18
good will...............................................................1
goose pimples .....................................................32
Grantham, Jeremy ..............................................24
group learning........................................................3
groups .....................5, 10, 11, 21-24, 42, 50, 72, 75
gut................................................18, 30-32, 34, 38

## H

Hirschman, Albert O...............................................8
hope ........................................... 1, 50, 65, 66, 72, 77
humor ................................................... 4, 18, 55

## I

inflexibility of positions .......................................14
inspiration ..................................... 7, 38, 67, 81, 93
international issues...............................................23
interpersonal strengths..........................................2
intuition ................................. 31-33, 37, 38, 43, 92
ISIS/ISIL/DAIISH.....................................................22

## J

Jobs, Steve ..........................................................33

## K

kindergarteners......................................................2

## L

learning curve........................................................8
limiting habits......................................................52
listening...............................................................55
longer-term goal...................................................65
lose power............................................................83
Luhrmann, T. M. ...................................................27
lying....................................................................73

## M

marriages ...............................................................8
meaning.............................................32, 38, 93, 95
methods .............................. 6, 18, 42, 43, 44, 51
Milgram, Stanley ....................................................7
misuse of power...................................................82

## N

negative emotions................................................37
negotiation ...........................................9-11,13-17,76
neurotransmitters ................................................31
new skills ...............................................2, 19, 76
nuclear proliferation ............................................23

## O

openness ..............................................................92
overdrive ..............................................................32

## P

pain ............................................................. 92-93
pamper yourself....................................................67
paradoxical information .......................................24
partnerships .....................................................8, 74
peace of mind.......................................................66
pecking orders........................................................7
physical activities .................................................67
plan ................................. 6, 44, 65, 75, 84, 85
positional bargaining............................................14
positive emotions.................................................37

poverty ....................................... 22

power ...................... 1, 28, 34, 47, 68, 80-81, 85-86

practice............................................ 55

practicing negotiating skills ............................... 19

problem complexity ............................ 41

problems related to work.................................... 37

processes for negotiation .................................... 16

## Q

Quiet Rage ....................................... 8

## R

realities......................................... 7

refocusing possibilities ......................... 32

relevant authority................................ 75

research methodology ........................ 44

resoluton ....................................... 11

resource depletion ............................. 22

results .............. 3, 8, 33, 38-39, 44-45, 51-52, 66, 76

rewards......................................... 81

Roosevelt, Franklin D............................... 43

## S

saboteurs....................................... 50

Sapolsky, Robert..................................... 7

Sartre, Jean Paul ................................... 27

self-fulfilling prophecy............................ 81

sense of humor........................................46, 50, 56

September 11 ................................... 22

sexual innuendo .................................. 73

significant issue ................................. 63

Simon, Herbert ................................... 32

social activities ................................. 76

Stanford Prison Experiment ................................. 8

stereotypes.......................................... 21

strategies......................................... 53

strengths......................... 2, 5, 7, 17, 44, 52, 54, 61

stressful events ...................................................... 7

styles of negotiation ............................................ 15

suffering................................................................ 92

synthesis .................................................. 24, 43, 44

## T

teach them to share in kindergarten ...................... 2

terrorism................................................................ 23

The Great Wave ................................................... 21

think for yourself ................................................. 27

third-parties .......................................................... 75

Thomas-Kilmann Conflict Mode Instrument......... 15

tools of communication....................................... 50

trends.............................................................. 23, 42

tribal issues .......................................................... 21

## U

unhealthy situations ............................................ 61

urban decay .......................................................... 22

uses of power ....................................................... 82

## V

victim .................................................................... 75

## W

*Wall Street Journal*................................ 7, 22, 32, 58

weapons proliferation ......................................... 22

whiny .................................................................... 75

work situations ...................................................... 8

## Z

Zimbardo, Philip.......................................................7

# APPENDIX A: DEFINITION OF COURAGE

# DEFINITION OF COURAGE

## DEFINITIONS FROM *CHOOSE COURAGE: STEP INTO THE LIFE YOU WANT*

### by Ruth M. Schimel, Ph.D., Career & Life Management Consultant

**Courage** is a process of becoming that involves:

- the willingness to realize your true capacities
- by going *through* discomfort, fear, anxiety, or suffering
- and taking wholehearted, responsible action

**Willingness** is the process of choosing unconditionally, voluntarily sacrificing alternatives.

**Realize** is to comprehend fully or correctly, to actualize or achieve.

**True** is consistent with reality, genuine, fundamental.

**Capacity** is the ability to hold, do, receive, or absorb; the maximum or optimum amount that can be achieved; the ability to learn or retain knowledge; a faculty or aptitude.

**Wholehearted** is to undertake fully with sincerity, openness to experience, compassion, and energy. It is something done for itself, not as a means to an end.

**Responsible** is being ethically accountable, accepting authorship.

**Action** is the process of doing, the transmission of energy, force, or influence as the result of responsible thought and intuition.

**Discomfort** is mental or bodily distress.

**Anxiety** is the state of unease and distress about future uncertainties, lacking an unambiguous cause or specific threat.

**Fear** is the feeling of alarm or disquiet caused by the expectation of specific danger, pain, or disaster.

**Suffering** is the feeling of actual pain or distress, sustaining of loss, injury, harm, or punishment; the enduring of evil, injury, pain, or death.

### Four Concepts Complementary to Courage

**Authenticity** is the process of realizing your genuine self through openness to yourself and others and receptivity to what you and others offer.

**Commitment** is the process of entrusting yourself to another person, idea, thing, or situation.

**Passion** is the range of emotions and desires, involving pain and pleasure, that focuses your energy for self-enactment.

**Vocation** is the idea or inspiration that gives meaning to your work. It is the calling that enables you to express who you are to yourself and others by producing something you value that also connects to a transcendent purpose.

# APPENDIX B: CYCLES OF COURAGE

# Three Cycles of Development in the Process of Becoming Courageous

"Becoming courageous is a process involving the willingness to realize your true capacities by going through discomfort, fear, anxiety or suffering and taking wholehearted, responsible action."

### First Cycle

- Wanting something very much expressed by having a passion and purpose
- Being aware of experiencing discomfort, anxiety, fear or suffering or feeling pain
- Taking support from others
- Believing in concrete, especially beneficial values
- Seeing reality

### Second Cycle

- Experiencing and naming a range of feelings
- Being willing to do work and endure pain, discomfort, or tension appropriate to a situation of value
- Making choices, letting go of some possibilities
- Taking appropriate, ethical action
- Gaining insight into and appreciation of your true self through learning, action and feedback from others
- Continuing the dialogue about what's important with yourself and others
- Taking good care of yourself

### Third Cycle

- Renewing periodically insights about yourself through life experience, dialogue, and contemplation
- Integrating true capacities, purpose, passion, and values in action
- Enjoying the ongoing creation of meaning in life
- Continuing to develop through the cycles and processes mentioned above

## Suggestions for use:

- Use and adapt what relates to your situation from the previous page.
- Identify several examples of your own process of becoming courageous by thinking of stories describing how you handled difficult or challenging situations.
- Listen to others' stories to parse out their process of becoming courageous in order to give them positive feedback. (Note: You may find yourself and others saying, "I had no choice," when you label action courageous.)

# About Ruth Schimel

**Career & Life Management Consulting Practice:** Ruth may not seem a neatly-defined expert to some people. Her focus is encouraging clients and readers to realize their true capacities for their own and others' benefit. To honor their complexity and variety, she integrates a range of ideas, subjects, and information, including the arts, social sciences, and sciences.

Since 1983, Ruth has consulted with over 1,000 career and life management clients of all ages and backgrounds. Building beyond conventional approaches, she provides extensive original materials, tools, and inspiration. Her tailored guidance elicits clients' uniqueness, while promoting self-sufficiency and progress. Ruth also speaks, trains, and facilitates groups.

The theme of courage that animates her practice reflects the focus of her doctoral dissertation which came unconventionally — through an image. It united her passions, interests, education, skills, and experience, just as she encourages her clients to do with their lives. From this research, she knows that dealing with a mob in Calcutta or confronting a street thief in Guatemala City was not courageous — probably foolhardy, in fact. But meaning what she says and doing what she means, as Horton the Elephant would say, comes closer to the spirit of her new, 21st-century definition of courage accessible to most people: *a process that involves the willingness to realize your true capacities by going **through** discomfort, fear, anxiety, or suffering and taking wholehearted, responsible action.*

**Author:** Since 2013, Ruth has published six books, starting with *Choose Courage: Step Into the Life You Want*. Subsequent related handbooks include themes of success and relationships. Her books are available through www.amazon.com under her name.

**Foundation and Nonprofit Work:** In 1998, Ruth developed with her mother and now leads and manages The Schimel Lode, a nontraditional foundation to promote collaboration and innovation for the public good in the Washington, D.C. area. The website is www.TheSchimelLode.net.

**Management Consulting and University Teaching:** Ruth continues as a management consultant for organizations. Previously, she taught a range of human resource and related subjects in the business schools at Georgetown and American Universities and for continuing education students at George Washington. She was an associate professor at Marymount University in the human resources master's program.

**Diplomacy:** As a diplomat, Ruth served at embassies in Ecuador and Guatemala, and as chief of the consular section in Calcutta, India. At the Department of State, she managed human resources and selection boards, analyzed research and intelligence, and worked on desks for Latin America countries. She continues to speak Spanish.

**Education:** Ruth's degrees are:

- Ph.D. in public management, workforce development, and gerontology, George Washington University (GWU): Dissertation topic: *Becoming Courageous: A Search for Process*

- M.A. in behavioral science, government, and personnel, GWU

- B.S. in industrial and labor relations, Cornell University

**© 2016. Ruth M. Schimel, Ph.D., Career & Life Management Consultant**

www.ruthschimel.com    ruth@ruthschimel.com    **202.659.1772**

# CHOOSE COURAGE SERIES BY RUTH M. SCHIMEL, PH.D.

# ORDER FORM

**Contact Ruth M. Schimel for Corporate Discounts and Bulk Purchases.**

Phone Order: 202-659-1772
Email Order: ruth@ruthschimel.com

To receive your books send your Checks or Money Orders to:

Ruth M. Schimel, Ph.D.
2555 Pennsylvania Avenue, NW, #514
Washington, DC 20037-1614

Please send my order to:

Person Ordering: _____
Organization Name: _____
Street Address: _____
City: _____ State_____
Postal Zone/ Zip Code _____ Email _____
Phone _____

BASIC ORDER:

Number of copies of:

_____ *Choose Courage: Step Into the Life You Want* (332 page, paperback book) $15.00

_____ *Choose Courage Step Into the Success You Want: Sparking Your Powers* (76 page paperback, Handbook #1) $5.00

_____ *Choose Courage Step Into the Success You Want: Building Bridges to Achievement* (78 page paperback, Handbook #2) $5.00

_____ *Choose Courage In Your Relationships: Empower Yourself First* (75 pages paperback, Handbook #3) $5.00

_____ *Choose Courage In Your Relationships: Thrive Together* (75 pages, Handbook #4) $5.00

_____ *Choose Courage In Your Relationships:Profit from Problems* (100 pages, Handbook #5) $5.00

Please add $3.00 for each shipment and $1.50 for each book for shipping and handling.

www.ingramcontent.com/pod-product-compliance
Lightning Source LLC
Chambersburg PA
CBHW080522030426

42337CB00023B/4596